CONFESSIONS OF A COMMUNITY COLLEGE ADMINISTRATOR

Matthew Reed

Foreword by Kay McClenney

insidehighered.com

JOSSEY-BASS
A Wiley Imprint
www.josseybass.com

Cover image: ©Jorgen Jacobsen/iStockphoto
Cover design: Michael Cook
Author photo: © Kimberly Deprey/Ravishing Photography

Published by Jossey-Bass
A Wiley Imprint
One Montgomery Street, Suite 1200, San Francisco, CA 94104-4594—www.josseybass.com

Jossey-Bass books and products are available through most bookstores. To contact Jossey-Bass
directly call our Customer Care Department within the U.S. at 800-956-7739, outside the U.S.
at 317-572-3986, or fax 317-572-4002.

Wiley publishes in a variety of print and electronic formats and by print-on-demand. Some
material included with standard print versions of this book may not be included in e-books or
in print-on-demand. If this book refers to media such as a CD or DVD that is not included in
the version you purchased, you may download this material at http://booksupport.wiley.com.
For more information about Wiley products, visit www.wiley.com.

Library of Congress Cataloging-in-Publication Data

ISBN 978-1-118-00473-9 (pbk.); ISBN 978-1-118-22172-3 (ebk.);
ISBN 978-1-118-23553-9 (ebk.); ISBN 978-1-118-26038-8 (ebk.)

Cataloging-in-Publication data has been applied for.

Printed in the United States of America
FIRST EDITION
PB Printing   10 9 8 7 6 5 4 3 2 1

CONTENTS

ABOUT THE AUTHOR

MATTHEW REED IS THE VICE PRESIDENT FOR ACADEMIC AFFAIRS at Holyoke Community College in Holyoke, Massachusetts. He was previously the division dean of liberal arts at the County College of Morris, New Jersey, and the dean of general education at DeVry University in North Brunswick, New Jersey. He has written the Confessions of a Community College Dean blog, as "Dean Dad," since 2004. He has taught at Rutgers University, Kean University, DeVry, and the County College of Morris. He has published articles in *New Political Science* and *Diversity Digest*, and won the Best Presentation award from the Undergraduate Education section of the American Political Science Association in 1999. He has a PhD in political science from Rutgers University and a BA from Williams College. He lives in Feeding Hills, Massachusetts, with his wife, Carolyn, their son, Kyle, and their daughter, Jessica.

ACKNOWLEDGMENTS

READERS, COWORKERS, AND LONGTIME FRIENDS HAVE BEEN WONDERFUL supporters over the years. Mike Greenfield and Bernard Tamas have been there since the beginning. Jeff Angus's "Management by Baseball" and Tedra Osell's "Bitch, Ph.D." were early role models. So many wonderful interlocutors have come and gone over the years, variously challenging me to rethink and encouraging the effort. Without their feedback, I would have dropped it all years ago.

Although they may not know or recognize their contributions, I'll ask the following to trust that their influence is here: Mary Aun, Barry Batorsky, Jack Becherer, Bettina Caluori, Jessica Chambers, Peter Conolly-Smith, Danielle Donders, Jim Dutcher, Nikki Edgecombe, Patrick Enright, Bill Fogarty, Linda Fogarty, Andrea Habura, Mark Hinrichs, Stephen Karlson, Dominic Latorraca, Herb Lebowitz, Aaron Levin, Sue Mackler, Lori Messinger, Bill Messner, Marcia Morrison, Mary Orisich, Tracy Ross, Anca Rosu, Bette Simmons, Idelia Smith, Bhupinder Sran, Linda Terranova, Wendolyn Tetlow, Yanina Vargas, and John Weber.

Scott Jaschik from InsideHigherEd.com came along at exactly the right moment and has been a wonderful support. My readers and commenters have taught me generously over the years; without their feedback, I likely would have dropped the whole enterprise in short order. David Brightman and Aneesa Davenport at Jossey-Bass were patient and encouraging as I struggled to make the transition from episodic to sustained writing. And Kay McClenney deserves special thanks for generously offering her time, words, and counsel.

My late father, Bill Reed, introduced me to academia through his own example. My mother, Kay Ford, toted barges and lifted bales to make it possible for me even to enter this profession, and has been a generous source of wisdom as I have struggled with all kinds of dilemmas. My brother, Brad Reed, slogged through an early draft of the manuscript and still speaks to me; I look forward to returning the favor.

And of course, Carolyn, Kyle, and Jessica—known on the blog as the Wife, the Boy, and the Girl—are the point of the whole enterprise. I thank them for putting up with me as I tried to fit the book in around a consuming day job, the blog, and the demands of parenthood. Without their regular reminders that there is more to life than work, I would have come unglued years ago.

FOREWORD

Kay McClenney

AMERICANS LIKE THEIR COMMUNITY COLLEGES. They particularly like the concept of *opportunity* afforded by these institutions. They believe that any American who is willing to work hard should have the opportunity to go to college. And remarkably, according to public opinion polling, many would be willing to pay additional taxes to ensure that community colleges continue to provide opportunity for all.

It seems that many people think of community colleges much as they do public utilities. You know they are there. You expect them to be available when you—or family members or neighbors or fellow citizens—need them: when a job is lost, when an affordable alternative to university tuition is the wise choice, when it's Mom's turn to further her education, when a new company moves to town and needs trained workers, when kids who haven't been challenged in high school need to learn how to be effective college students, when small classes and personal attention are key to educational success.

Yet beyond holding these philosophical and utilitarian values, the general public understands little about how community colleges operate, how they are financed (or not), and what the challenges are in the work of making postsecondary education available in this country, with commitment to quality *and* affordability, for a wildly diverse student population. People also are typically surprised to learn that community colleges enroll close to half (44 percent) of the undergraduate students in the United States.

Unfortunately, these shortages of understanding all too often extend even into the ranks of higher education. Contrary to still-common belief, community colleges are not extensions of high schools and are not mis-shapen universities. They are not places where faculty and administrators are willing to sacrifice academic excellence for access—rather, they want both. These colleges are not, emphatically, places only for somebody else's kids.

Community colleges in this century are the gateway to the American middle class. They are the country's best hope for reversing the U.S.

decline in educational attainment relative to other developed countries
and for restoring losses in average family income. Recognizing this reality,
a plethora of players—from the White House to the State House to the
philanthropic community and the kitchen table—are taking community
colleges more seriously than at any point in their one-hundred-plus-year
history. The colleges are on the receiving end of welcome attention and
sometimes uncomfortable scrutiny. The country needs them, and more
than a few people wonder if they can step up and measure up.

It's an open question and one that Matthew Reed takes on in this
timely and useful book, seeking to help prepare the next generation of
administrators and leaders for the challenges, large and small, that they
must face. Despite the size of the community college sector (more than
eleven hundred institutions serving over 7.5 million credit students), few
young people envision a career in these colleges, whether as faculty members, student services professionals, or administrators. Many find their
way to the colleges serendipitously or through part-time positions or by
following their values. The career paths often are long and winding roads,
filled with the sharp curves and potholes of learning by doing.

Furthermore, just at the time when community and societal needs for
community colleges are at an all-time high, the institutions (like other
employment sectors) face massive turnover as baby boomers retire. An
estimated 75 percent of current community college CEOs say that they
plan to retire within the decade, according to the American Association
of Community Colleges. And the "pipeline" positions—typically vice
presidencies and provosts—are similarly populated with people nearing
retirement age. Finding and developing women and men to assume leadership of community colleges, from midlevel to the top, knowing what
they need to do and willing to do it, are critical priorities.

Fondly known to many readers only as "Dean Dad," a pseudonym
used as author of a popular *Inside Higher Ed* blog, Matthew Reed
arrived on the national community college scene at an important junc-
ture. Writing directly from the front lines of administration, he illumi-
nates the work of managing and leading community colleges, describing
with clarity and pathos, exasperation and humor, what it really entails.
Yet his eyes rise from the mundane to the meaningful, from the problem
in front of us to the much larger challenge on the horizon.

Reed begins the book by stating a solemn and accurate pair of truths:
that community colleges face daunting challenges that they currently
are not designed to meet, and that sustaining the key mission of these
institutions—open access, with quality and affordability—is crucial to the

society. Then, for the benefit both of those who seek to lead and those who seek to understand what leadership means in a dramatically changing environment, he peels the onion.

In the first two chapters, he provides context for the work of community college administration. Chapter One describes multiple missions, often competing with one another; low tuition; low prestige; and perpetual underfunding to do some of the most difficult work in education. Then Reed insists that the administrator's job is to "make none of that matter." Good start! Then he moves in Chapter Two to a more detailed exploration of the funding challenges of community colleges, destined to become not less but more acute in the future, especially if leaders take a business-as-usual approach.

Moving from context to daily reality, Reed uses the next three chapters to describe in concrete and occasionally ironic terms what academic deans and other administrators at community colleges actually do and the human, political, and organizational challenges they confront. No sugarcoating here, but illumination of real dynamics in real places. Sometimes it may sound like fiction, but it isn't.

Chapter Six ends the book as it must, by addressing some fundamentals of community college design, questioning whether they are suited to the future, and concluding that they very likely are not. Again using real examples, Reed demonstrates the axiom that community colleges, like other organizations, are perfectly designed to produce precisely the results they are currently getting. Currently, those results are not good enough— for students, their communities, or the nation. And Reed offers constructive, even if also disruptive, alternatives.

His writing brings common sense, compassion, civility, and courage to dilemmas of daily work and to questions of institutional purpose, form, and viability. It is a voice we need, and just in time.

Kay McClenney is director of the Center for Community College Student Engagement and senior lecturer in the Community College Leadership Program at the University of Texas at Austin.

INTRODUCTION

I TAKE IT AS GIVEN THAT THE AMERICAN COMMUNITY COLLEGE in its current form is unsustainable. But I also take it as given that the purpose of the community college—providing high-quality education and training on a mass scale at low cost—has never been more important.

The next generation of community college leaders has its work cut out for it. If they wish to survive, community colleges will have to adapt in pretty dramatic ways. If they don't, they will become increasingly ineffective and irrelevant, and their irrelevance will create a space for actors with other agendas to step in. It's up to the next cohort of leaders to make some fundamental choices.

Most of the public has very little understanding of the issues behind institutional sustainability. It sees ever-escalating costs and wonders what colleges are thinking. Most of the people within higher education have very little understanding of sustainability, either, though for different reasons. They see cascading budget cuts and wonder what administrators (or the public) are thinking.

The generation currently aging out of community college leadership came up in a very different time. From 1960 to 1970, the United States added 497 community colleges; that's almost exactly one per week for a decade. In the forty-plus years since, it has added less than half that many. Faculty employment has grown tremendously, but only in the ranks of the part-time and nonbenefited. State shares of budgets have dropped steadily for decades, with severe acceleration following the economic crash of 2008. For-profit providers, once marginal presences, now account for one out of every nine undergraduates in America, and their share continues to grow (Vaughan, 2006).

The game has changed, but community colleges are still playing by the old rules.

The leaders who came up in better times have a way of waiting for the better times to return. They've perfected a cycle of retrench-refill-retrench that leaves the underlying structure more or less intact. Every year you replace only about half of the faculty who retire or leave, using adjuncts for the rest; you cut travel and professional development at each new recession; and you raise tuition faster than inflation, consoling yourself that financial aid will make it okay.

If it weren't obvious already, the aftermath of the 2008 crash has made it clear that the strategy of hold-your-breath-until-the-money-comes-back is exhausted.

Paradoxically, the moment at which community colleges are more threatened than they have ever been is also the moment at which they're more needed than ever. Presidents Bush and Obama both singled out community colleges in their State of the Union addresses for playing key roles in training and retraining the workforce. Total student loan debt recently surpassed total credit card debt in the United States; in that setting, community colleges' niche as low-cost providers is more important than ever.

Community college administrators saw the paradox on the ground. In 2009, for example, my college hit a new enrollment record with a recession-driven double-digit percentage increase in students *at the exact same time* that it sustained the largest state aid cut in its history. In a situation like that, the structural flaws of the organization become impossible to ignore. A for-profit business—whether in education or anything else—experiences growth as a revenue source. But for a college that sells its product at less than the cost of production, by design, growth is a cost. In California, they deal with that by simply refusing to grow; enrollment caps and wait lists are the order of the day. In my neck of the woods, we dealt with that by scrambling for innovation and cutting administration and building maintenance. We got through the enrollment surge—it's coming down to more normal levels again—but we still don't have a plan for long-term sustainability. Eventually, all those heroically long days and forever-deferred costs catch up to you.

The current leadership of community colleges is not sustainable, either. The average age of college presidents has climbed steadily over the past few decades as the founding generation has largely aged in place. In 1986, 14 percent of college presidents were age sixty-one or older; as of 2011, 58 percent of college presidents were (Cook and Kim, 2012). Chief academic officers—still the most common feeder job for presidents—aren't far behind, and fewer of them express interest in presidencies than once did. Although I haven't seen good statistics on deans and midlevel academic administrators, on-the-ground observation suggests that much the same dynamic holds.

As a result, we can expect that strapped colleges will be increasingly in need of thoughtful new leadership in the next decade.

The next generation that steps in will find a unique set of challenges. Societal expectations of community colleges far outstrip the political willingness to fund them. Role expectations—such as tenure—that were based on easier times have become obstacles to change. Internal political imperatives on campus run directly counter to external trends, and people who dare to say so are often shown the door. But as a coping strategy, denial has exhausted its usefulness.

This book is intended to orient the next generation of community college leadership to the new realities. It's written in the tragic hope of the reformer. My goal here, to steal a line from FDR, is to bend community colleges so they don't break.

It's a difficult mission on a good day. Internal constituencies often don't want to hear about necessary change; they've done well enough, thank you very much, and would prefer just to be left alone. And the outside world's attention span and patience for detail don't lend themselves to nuanced approaches. But if you believe in the mission of public higher education—which I do, strongly—then you can't afford to fetishize particular institutional arrangements.

If we don't reform community colleges meaningfully, they'll eventually go the way of other mid-twentieth-century institutions. They'll succumb to more class-stratified and expensive alternatives, leaving people who want inexpensive access to higher education without an option. People who can afford premium tuition can always find what they want; the rest will be consigned to a panoply of do-it-yourself options of varying quality and relevance in the marketplace. The idea of public higher education—delivering the best to everyone, regardless of ability to pay—will be sacrificed to the internal interest-group politicking of its last incumbents. No, thanks.

The next group to step up won't have the option of just waiting for the money to come back. It will have to make some significant changes. My goal here is to help that next group understand what it's up against, how to manage in the meantime, and how best to make constructive change—the kind that subordinates this institutional form or that one to the mission—more likely.

Parents' Day

An exchange at home, with my (then) six-year-old daughter:
  "Daddy, what did you do at work today?"
  "Well, I had a bunch of meetings."
  "But what did you *do*?"

A few months later, she invited me to "career day" at her school, to try to explain to her first-grade class just what it is that I do all day. The best I could come up with was "I try to get grown-ups to play nice and share their toys." They looked puzzled, and I quickly turned it over to my friend the chemical engineer, who explained molecules by dancing among the chairs.

College administration is a tricky endeavor, especially on the academic side of the operation. (My experience has been on the academic side, and the academic side will be the focus of this book. Deans of human resources or admissions have different challenges, and I'll leave discussion of those to people who know that terrain.) As with any hard-to-explain job, misconceptions abound—some rooted in good faith, some rooted in other agendas.

Having spent over a decade in academic administration, most of it at community colleges, I've had to learn on the job. My career was a function of happenstance. I didn't set out to go into administration; my PhD is in a social science discipline, and my plan all along was to become a tenured professor in my field at a charming liberal arts college somewhere, teaching bright young minds until retirement. But the world had other plans.

What I Try to Do

In a community college setting, deans (or associate deans, depending on context) are in a difficult position. They don't set macro policies, which come instead from the president, the board, or both. But they're identified by the faculty as part of the administration, so any animus toward any given policy will get directed their way, whether they agree with the policy or not.

In the settings in which I've worked, the faculty have been tenured and unionized, and the deans were not eligible for either. When tenured faculty moved into deanships, which sometimes happened, they had to give up tenure and their faculty rank. Unsurprisingly, finding acceptable and capable candidates who are willing to give up tenure, union protections, summer vacations, four-day schedules, and casual dress codes for remarkably small pay increases and jobs that offer responsibility without authority is often an uphill battle.

That said, though, there are real satisfactions inherent in academic administration, and people who can do the job well make valuable contributions.

The core job of the academic administrator, whatever her title, is to help set the background conditions in which faculty and staff can do their best work.

That's far more complicated than it sounds. Background conditions can encompass all sorts of factors, from material conditions to even-handed applications of rational rules to defensible judgment calls to basic interpersonal trust. And the options available are always constrained by various sorts of scarcity, legacy choices, local culture, and the sheer diversity of personalities involved. Even the best deans have to say no a lot.

Doing the job well requires a rare blend of skills. It requires firsthand knowledge of the reality of the classroom, preferably of the sort gained by years of full-time teaching. It requires an intuitive sense of the quirks of academic culture, which are often inscrutable to people coming from, say, business or military environments. It requires skill and patience with budgets. It requires significant diplomatic skills, and sometimes a talent for political infighting. (Generally, though, if it requires more infighting than diplomacy, then it's time to find another place to work.) And increasingly, it requires a fairly advanced sense of external political and economic conditions.

On a personal level, it requires self-discipline and self-awareness. Some professors who are absolutely wonderful in the classroom—where they get to be the undisputed authority—are simply awful as administrators, where they have to collaborate and often subordinate their own egos or preferences to others. The professor is paid to be the smartest person in the room when teaching; sometimes he forgets to take that hat off in other settings. The dean is not paid to be the smartest person in the room, and needs to avoid the temptation to slip into old habits.

It's easy for deans to fail. Too much ego will lead to decisions made for the wrong reasons. Too little will lead to chaos, as strong-willed faculty subordinate institutional needs to their own preferences when the dean is afraid to say no. Inattention to detail can lead to disaster, and inattention to the big picture can lead to decisions that miss the point of the rules.

Community colleges don't have clear and discernible "bottom lines" in the sense that businesses do. As publicly supported nonprofits with missions to serve the public good, there's often a swarm of different criteria flying around at any given time, bumping into each other. Which is better, high pass rates or high standards? Efficiency or innovation? I wouldn't trust anyone who could give a blanket answer to either of those questions; context matters. The dean has to be able to make judgment calls with partial information, choosing from among imperfect options, in a setting in which her critics will have even less information and, sometimes, life tenure. It's not easy.

This book is written in recognition and in hope. In recognition that colleges work better when the people in management roles know what they're doing and do it well. Tolstoy famously wrote that happy families are all alike, but that unhappy families are each unhappy in their own way. Academic administrators are subject to a version of that. Failures are conspicuous, but success goes almost unnoticed; things just sort of work. And I write in hope that the next generation of managers will manage not only what's there but also the transition to what could be.

My Story

My experience in higher education is idiosyncratic. I attended a well-respected small liberal arts college as an undergrad, graduating with honors. I moved to a flagship public university for graduate school, earning a doctorate in a traditional academic discipline in the social sciences, fully intending to become a professor at a college similar to the one I attended. While there, I worked as a teaching assistant in my own discipline, but I also spent two years as a teaching assistant in the English department, teaching several sections of freshman composition. Then I graduated into the sausage-grinder academic job market of the mid-1990s.

By that time, the assumptions underlying graduate placement had largely collapsed. In graduate school, fellowships and teaching assistantships were allocated on the assumption that the student would apply for, and get, a job while ABD (all-but-dissertation). But the market had shifted by then, so colleges could afford to look only at candidates with the PhD in hand. That meant that students fell off a cliff upon graduation: their graduate programs expected them to have a job in hand before leaving, and employers expected them to have the degree in hand before applying. By the time I graduated, I had spent a couple of years unsuccessfully looking for a full-time job, and my departmental funding had run out.

I vividly remember standing in the auditorium after the graduation ceremony, degree in hand, wondering just what the hell I was going to do next. I didn't have a job at that point, and my graduate funding had run out. For a few months, it wasn't at all clear how I'd even support myself. After all those years of grad student poverty, I suddenly faced the real thing. It was hard not to ask myself some tough questions. Some of those nights were long.

That summer, I joined the ranks of the "freeway fliers," adjuncts who cobble together a meager living by driving from one part-time teaching job to another, being paid by the course. I drove an hour each way in a hatchback without air conditioning to a storefront operation that taught SAT preparation to fourteen-year-olds. I also picked up a pair of adjunct English classes at a nearby for-profit college—call it For-Profit U (FPU for short). When summer ended, the SAT prep course ended with it, but I picked up an adjunct class at "Flagship State."

As fall approached, though, I was able to parlay my adjunct job at FPU into a full-time faculty position there. Oddly enough, the English composition experience I had in graduate school was the key; unlike many people, I could teach a range of disciplines. Because FPU was expanding rapidly at that point, I made an attractive hire: I was credentialed, I was cheap, I could teach a wide range of subjects, and I had already shown as an adjunct that I knew more or less what I was doing.

FPU was an unusual academic employer, and not only because it was for-profit. The teaching calendar was twelve months: three four-month "trimesters." Faculty taught fifteen credits per trimester, twelve months a year, for an annual load of forty-five credits. For the sake of comparison, community college faculty in that state carried annual loads of thirty credits, and the lowest-level four-year colleges required annual loads of twenty-four. Forty-five was backbreaking, and effectively crowded out the time needed to publish my way back into contention for the jobs I had in mind when I started graduate school.

Despite the arduous teaching load—and students who had chosen FPU specifically to avoid anything that resembled a liberal arts class—FPU was able to attract a surprisingly strong young faculty in short order. The "great wave of retirements" that Bowen and Sosa (1989) predicted would materialize by that point and generate great demand for tenure-track faculty had crashed on the shoals of reality, and an entire generation of graduate students came to grief in a market that only wanted them as adjuncts. (Since then, this trend has only worsened.) Because FPU was geographically close to Flagship State, it was able to attract some hot young PhD's without paying much; even with a backbreaking teaching load, a full-time job there was vastly preferable to adjuncting at more prestigious places. As many of us noticed, you can't eat prestige.

Note the irony here: the for-profit sector offered a real job, whereas the nonprofits offered only adjunct work. The stereotype is that the for-profits are wildly exploitative and the nonprofits virtuous and kind; the truth is somewhat less black and white. Had the nonprofits stepped up, my career would have taken a very different direction.

At the time I was hired, FPU was beefing up its PhD faculty as part of convincing the state to allow it to offer bachelor's degrees. That meant that it recruited a cohort of young faculty enculturated in traditional academia, and threw us into an organization designed to be anything but. The culture clashes were frequent and wearing; several of us hired during this period referred to our cohort as the Island of Misfit Toys. FPU was unapologetically vocational in its orientation, and it attracted students who reflected that. Its home office leadership was clearly focused on the bottom line, and it treated the "general education" classes as curiosities. Yes, they needed to run, and yes, they were actually fairly profitable, but the home office had little to no interest in them.

I spent several years at FPU in my faculty role. I taught courses across a range of liberal arts disciplines, including but not limited to my own. In my time there, students never had the option of majoring in anything I taught, so I had to learn to reach students who had no idea why they had to take my class. On the best days there were breakthroughs, but I have to admit that frustration was never far from the surface.

A Road Less Traveled

After a few years on faculty, I started to realize that I wasn't going to write my way out of FPU—I was just too exhausted from all that teaching—and I didn't want to burn out in the classroom. I recall the conversation I had with my dean, in which I told him that I was interested in picking up some administrative work as a way of diversifying my workload. He looked at me incredulously.

"You actually *want* administrative work?"

I assured him that I did.

Not a week later, I was tapped as coordinator of the campus accreditation self-study.

That was an education in itself, and a good introduction to administrative work. I got a crash course in outcomes assessment and a crash course in the realities of trying to corral faculty around a project that many of them considered ancillary, if not entirely contrived.

From there, I worked briefly as a curriculum coordinator, the rough equivalent of a department chair in that context. The moment that stuck with me in that role came from the then-director of the career services office, which held a key role at FPU. He had asked me for some information about teaching schedules, and I got it to him the next day. He commented to my dean that he had never had quick and accurate turnaround on a request for anything from faculty before, and that he found it refreshing. As my dean dryly noted, "that's administration."

Shortly thereafter, an associate dean position opened, and I went for it. It was a full-time administrative position with no assigned teaching responsibilities, though we were allowed (and even encouraged) to do an adjunct course at night.

A year later, my dean decamped for a position at a newly opened campus of FPU, and I moved into his old role.

By that point, FPU's enrollment had started a sharp decline. The technology bubble had burst, and the appeal of a telecommunications degree had suddenly evaporated. Home office responded with a series of initiatives that I considered ill-advised, if not offensive. I could see that the longer I stayed, the more I would have to take responsibility for decisions with which I fundamentally disagreed. So I started applying for deanships at other colleges.

In 2003, I accepted a dean of liberal arts position at a nearby community college. I've worked in the world of community college administration ever since.

Careful What You Wish For

The deanship was a wonderful learning experience, but much of what I had absorbed at FPU didn't really carry over to the new job. My new world was tenured, unionized, and far, far older than the one I had left. Worse, the vice president to whom I reported had so much history with so many people at that point that I quickly became more or less irrelevant. Out of frustration and boredom, I started a blog in 2004, and began posting daily under the title Confessions of a Community College Dean in 2005. I used the pseudonym "Dean Dad" because those two roles defined most of my waking hours, and, drawing on the lessons of feminism, I wanted to highlight the work-life issues that were so real to me on a daily basis. The blog "turned pro" in 2007, when InsideHigherEd.com picked it up as a regular feature. It has been a venue for reflection (and discussion with my wise and worldly readers) on the state of higher education, how we got here, and what the alternatives might be. I've kept the title even though I moved to another community college as a vice president for academic affairs in 2008.

Organization of the Book

I start with some basic convictions:

- An educated citizenry is inherently a good idea for reasons both economic and moral.
- The open-door admissions policy that defines community colleges in the United States is a public good.

- The economic pressures that have intensified on both public higher education and the middle class generally will continue and further intensify for the foreseeable future.

- For-profit colleges and universities are not going away anytime soon, even as their political fortunes wax and wane.

As the next generation of leaders moves into place, it will encounter many of the same issues I did. I hope that this book helps these future leaders step back from the day-to-day struggles a bit and gain some perspective on the larger picture. Ideally, it will help them figure out the most useful and productive directions for constructive change.

The first two chapters provide institutional context.

To understand why things work (or don't work) the way they do, you have to have a sense of how they are put together. To that end, Chapter One, The Community College Landscape, outlines the deeply conflicted expectations that have taken root in many community colleges. Briefly, that chapter argues that many of the basic organizing principles of community colleges don't mesh well together because they were taken piecemeal from different contexts. Put together, they create strange and painful tensions that often defeat necessary and productive reforms. Because the principles were never really coherent, they've given rise, both necessarily and unintentionally, to their opposites on the ground: for example, distance education makes service areas problematic.

Chapter Two, Funding: Where the Money Comes From, Where It Goes, and Why There's Never Enough, addresses the economic framework within which most community colleges work. It outlines what I take to be the central economic dilemma facing public higher education: the inability to improve its own productivity. With that as background, the chapter details the drivers behind the seemingly contradictory trends of ever higher tuition and ever more adjuncts. It explains why it's easier to fund a new building than to fund people to teach in it.

The next two chapters address the daily reality of community college administration.

Chapter Three, Community College Administration: Who Does What, shifts the focus from the institutional setting of college administration to the daily reality of college administration. Drawing on years of firsthand experience, it gives a sense of the things that academic deans and other administrators at community colleges actually do.

Chapter Four, Herding Cats: Managing Creative People, addresses the basic dilemma of managing creative people who often don't think they even have managers. The eternal challenge is to keep people working together well without squelching the creativity that makes them valuable in the first place. Chapter Five, Regular Challenges of the Dean's Job, is an unfortunately far from exhaustive overview of other dilemmas deans must confront. New challenges come along every year, and each setting has its own idiosyncrasies, but the chapter gives a sense of some of the most common causes of administrative headaches. I hope that aspiring administrators find this chapter particularly useful.

The last chapter steps back from the day-to-day, and offers the beginnings of discussion of positive change.

Chapter Six, Saving Community Colleges: A Few Modest Proposals, turns to emergent and possible external alternatives to community colleges as they currently exist. Here I draw on my own experience as both a full-time faculty member and academic dean in a major for-profit university, as well as on the trends of the last several years, to show in realistic terms what else can happen.

The chapter also suggests internal changes that, if undertaken quickly and purposefully, could help public higher education adapt to the changes that have taken place in the decades since the building boom stopped. Many of these suggestions are vulnerable to charges of political difficulty, of course, but I think it would be immoral to let difficulty become fatalism. Too much is riding on community colleges to simply let them wither on the vine.

Within academic culture, we have an unfortunate tendency to address every dilemma as far too complex for description and then to throw up our hands and decide that nothing can be done. That tendency is grounded in an obvious truth: of course the world contains things far beyond our philosophy. But fatalism is selfish. People need education, and community colleges are uniquely situated to help millions of people and the economy as a whole. Imperfect and partial improvements matter. The world will keep changing whether we academics give it permission or not; we'd be well advised to participate in shaping those changes.

THE COMMUNITY
COLLEGE LANDSCAPE

COMMUNITY COLLEGES DON'T GET MUCH RESPECT. We all know the stereotypes: thirteenth grade, "high school with ashtrays," the place you go when you can't get in anyplace else. The ashtrays are mostly gone now, but the other stereotypes linger. And there is some truth to them. Yes, most community colleges have open-door admissions policies, which means that anyone with a high school diploma or GED can get in. (Until 2012, you didn't even need those; students who lacked either could take an "ability to benefit" test and get in that way.) Yes, many community colleges do a great deal of "developmental" (formerly called "remedial") instruction, filling in gaps that were supposed to have been covered in high school. Tuition tends to be markedly lower at community colleges than in any other sector of higher education, so the folks who equate price with quality will leap to certain conclusions. Community colleges tend not to draw national superstars to the faculty, simply by virtue of teaching loads and salaries. And "comprehensive" or "technical" community colleges often teach subjects that traditional colleges don't, whether that means auto repair, dental hygiene, or English as a Second Language.

Paradoxically, though, community colleges have never mattered more. Presidents Bush and Obama both mentioned them by name in State of the Union addresses, hailing their potential as job training centers for workers whose jobs have been displaced by automation and globalization. When the accumulated student loan debt in the United States passed the level of accumulated credit card debt, and the Occupy movement started to make hay about student loans, community colleges stood out as an obvious alternative for students who didn't want to overspend on an education (Cauchon, 2011). Nationally, community college enrollments hit unprecedented levels in the wake of the 2008–2009 recession as adults sought job retraining, and recent high school graduates sought affordability.

Although community colleges are still generally considered outside the academic prestige hierarchy, they're being called on to serve more people in more ways than they have in the past. And in many cases, they're being asked to do it with less per-student funding than they've ever had, controlling for inflation.

Community college administrators have the challenge of managing increasingly complicated organizations with conflicting missions, considerable internal politics, and chronic funding constraints. And they have to do it in a setting in which the political climate is both anti-tax and pro-"accountability." They have the additional challenge of working with a powerful constituency—faculty—whose demands are almost always for increasing costs, at the exact same time that they're working in an external environment demanding cost controls.

It isn't easy.

Diffuse Missions

To have any chance of reasonable success in managing a college, it's important to know what the college's goals are. Although every college has its own mission statement, most community college missions fall along one or several of the following lines.

Transfer

This is the old "junior college" model, in which a student would take the first two years of a four-year degree and then transfer. Although this is often the least recognized element of the community college mission in our political discourse, transfer-oriented majors are often the largest majors on campus. (At both of the community colleges at which I've worked, the generic "liberal arts transfer" major was, by far, the highest-enrolled program on campus.) The transfer function is particularly popular among students of traditional college age.

The "start here, finish there" model has real appeal. At a basic level, it's generally much cheaper than starting as a freshman at a four-year college, even within the public sector. Most community colleges don't have dorms, so the vast majority of the students commute. (There's a growing group of online students, but that's another discussion.) Living at home and paying low tuition can reduce or eliminate the debt burden that a student would otherwise have to assume, at least for the first two years. It can also be a boon to students who have family issues that require their continued presence, for students who have children of their own, or for students (or parents) who fear the perceived depravities of dorm life. For students who are eligible for Pell grants—a federal program that helps needy students pay for college—it's not unusual for the grant to cover the full cost of tuition. (At most four-year schools, the grant falls well short of the total cost.) That way, they only have to borrow for the last two years of a four-year degree.

The transfer function is also a second chance for the student whose high school transcript reflects indifferent or even terrible performance. Nothing proves the ability to succeed in college as well as actual success in college, so it can make sense for a student whose high school career fell short of his real talents to start fresh at a community college, establish a strong record there, and subsequently get a transfer scholarship based on success at the community college. I've seen many students capitalize on that second chance, and it still strikes me as one of the strongest arguments for community colleges. Second chances matter, and the combination of open admissions and a clear transfer route offers students a second chance they can actually use.

Unfortunately for many community colleges, the transfer route doesn't always look the way that most people imagine it looks. In theory, a student arrives in September as a freshman, takes two years of credit-bearing classes, graduates, and then starts at a four-year college as a junior. And that does happen.

But exceptions are more common than the rule. Many students arrive that first September (or January) needing remediation in English, math, or both. That adds time to the degree path and dramatically reduces the likelihood of graduation. Some attend on a part-time basis, usually for economic reasons; doing so stretches out the time to degree completion and reduces the likelihood of graduation. (The longer the path, the more opportunities there are for life to get in the way.) Other students arrive only ever intending to take one year before transferring. In those cases, there's frequently a deal between the parents and the student: spend a year at community college to show that you're serious, and if your grades are good enough, we'll send you to the four-year college you really wanted. That makes sense from the student's perspective, and it's quite common, but it shows up in the college's statistics as attrition. At the state level, it's interpreted as the community college having failed, even if the student goes on to successfully complete a four-year degree. (The federal Integrated Postsecondary Education Data System [IPEDS] data, which is the industry standard source for attrition, counts only "first-time, full-time, degree-seeking" students. At most community colleges, the IPEDS cohort is a distinct minority.)

Remediation

It's no secret that many prospective students arrive at college lacking the academic skills necessary to succeed at college-level work. Selective colleges and universities handle that by simply refusing admission to those students. But community colleges, by dint of their mission, don't have that option.

Remediation is often treated as the dirty little secret of community colleges. It has long been common practice for the full-time faculty in English and math departments to crowd themselves into upper-level courses as much as possible, and to push the developmental courses onto adjuncts. That's individually rational—people trained as college math professors often envisioned themselves teaching more differential equations than arithmetic, and they just can't bring the same passion to the latter as to the former—but systemically perverse; the most vulnerable students often encounter the least experienced (and least institutionally supported) instructors.

Developmental courses don't count toward graduation or degrees, though they do count for financial aid purposes. They're typically based on a "skills deficit" model, in which students' diagnosed deficiencies are addressed one at a time for as long as it takes.

Developmental instruction has a terrible image problem, and its stigma does harm to the public standing of community colleges generally. Politicians looking to cut spending will ask why they're paying for a college to reteach material that was (or should have been) covered in the K–12 sector. As developmental sequences have grown longer—to address ever deeper diagnosed skills deficits—student resentment at having to take the courses has increased. Worse, recent research has shown a disturbing lack of correlation between placement test results and subsequent success in college coursework, and a surprisingly high success rate in college-level work for students who "placed" developmental but somehow managed to evade the developmental coursework (Roksa, Jenkins, Jaggars, Zeidenberg, and Cho, 2009).

For emerging community college leaders, this is an area where it's possible to make a dramatic difference quickly. Although each party to the debate has its own reasons, there's significant consensus that community colleges need to do a better job of getting students into college-level courses. Making real progress in this area would be a great foundation for an administrator's career and a great service to the students and taxpayers.

Workforce Development

This has long been a part of the mission for comprehensive and vocational community colleges. (A comprehensive community college embraces both vocational and transfer-oriented programs.) Whether these programs are credit bearing or noncredit, the idea behind workforce development programs is to equip students with the skills to get the jobs that are out there, or to move up the ladder within a given company or career track.

Politically, this element of the community college mission is the most popular. It offers an answer to the question of what to do about jobs and economic development. And there's no question that in some cases, it meets real needs in a concrete way. The adult student who used to work at a factory that has since closed and who goes to the local community college to get retrained as a nurse will be much better off than if that training didn't exist.

Of course, many of the classic liberal arts programs have some workforce development elements to them, too. At the selective liberal arts college I attended, where talk of learning for its own sake was part of the culture, it was widely understood that many of us would move on subsequently to professional education, whether in the form of law school, medical school, or graduate school. Vocationalism wasn't absent; it was merely postponed.

By that same argument, one could easily define the transfer function as a form of workforce development. The student who starts at the local community college, transfers for a four-year degree, and then goes on to medical school—and yes, those students exist—will do quite well economically, thank you very much. Given that many of the higher-paying jobs require four-year or even graduate degrees, one would think that transfer would be a cornerstone of workforce development.

But in the larger political discourse, workforce development isn't understood that way. It's usually presented as an alternative to more "academic" programs. In the political discussion, the ideal workforce development program is short term, narrow, and cheap, and it turns the unemployable into the well employed.

The tension between the more expansive definition and the more crimped one often plays itself out on campus, where the liberal arts faculty often regard workforce programs with suspicion, and the workforce program faculty sometimes regard the liberal arts faculty as effete snobs. When resources are tight and a new position going to program A means no new position for program B, some degree of that tension is probably inevitable. But it's the job of the administrator to make sure that whatever rivalries may develop don't become dysfunctional or distracting.

Workforce development programs are also, by necessity, subject to the shifting winds of the economy. Demand for the programs tends to be highest when the number of job openings is lowest, and vice versa. Depending on the specificity of the training, too, the student who benefits this year may be back a few years later when the company has been bought, has gone under, or has been downsized. Because the availability of workforce programs is often dependent on the availability of grant funding, there are times when the training programs are either in front of, or behind, employer demand, and program graduates can't find work.

The most successful programs are often those that target incumbent workers and help them keep up with evolving technology or protocols in their fields. Frequently, companies will contract with a college to run an entire class on the company's premises. When the courses don't carry academic credit, they aren't bound by the usual rules around seat time, so they can be configured to meet specific needs.

Community Colleges in the Hierarchy of Higher Education

Every profession has its hierarchies, and academia is no exception.

In many for-profit industries, the relevant ranking may be by either market share or net profits. A company with a growing customer base and a healthy bottom line is considered to be doing well, whatever the quality of its products or services.

In higher education, though, profit is still considered somewhat suspect, and size doesn't tell you much. For example, Williams College with its two thousand students is considered far more prestigious than Arizona State University with its fifty thousand students. The relevant currency in academia is prestige, and prestige rests on both funding and exclusivity. The harder it is to get into a college, the thinking goes, the better the education must be. Never join a club that would accept you as a member.

Community colleges don't do well on either funding or exclusivity, so they don't do well in the status hierarchy.

In some ways, that doesn't matter much. The most prestigious colleges and universities recruit nationally and even internationally, so Harvard in Massachusetts and Stanford in California often compete for the same students. Community colleges tend to be devoted to single service areas—sometimes called "districts"—and generally don't do much recruiting outside those areas. (Online courses are an interesting, emerging exception. More on those later.) There might be some rivalry in towns that border service areas, and occasionally some programmatic specialization that will lure students into neighboring territory, but the bulk of the student body is geographically close to campus. Among other things, that means that Monroe Community College in Rochester, New York, doesn't have to wonder how it stacks up against Washtenaw Community College in Ann Arbor, Michigan; for all intents and purposes, the comparison is irrelevant.

The lack of prestige that attaches to community colleges attaches to them as an entire sector. In fact, in many ways, people's attitudes toward community colleges are similar to their attitudes toward Congress: they don't much like the group overall, but they like their own representative or campus just fine.

Community colleges' redheaded stepchild position within American higher education is both odd and understandable. It's odd in the sense that over 40 percent of the undergraduate students in the United States at any given time are enrolled at community colleges (Vaughn, 2006). That's a far higher percentage than are enrolled, say, at research universities. It's passing strange to describe such a large plurality as the aberration and to take narrow niches of higher education—such as the Ivies—as the norm.

But it's understandable against the backdrop of their origin stories. Many community colleges actually started out as outgrowths of public high schools. (That's why many of them have service "districts," modeled on K–12 school districts. Some of them even have "superintendents," in the manner of K–12 districts.) Others began as personal fiefdoms for failed politicians, or as sideline hobbies for faculty at four-year colleges. (For example, Holyoke Community College, in Massachusetts, was started by moonlighting faculty from Mount Holyoke and Smith Colleges.) Although most have grown far beyond their modest origins, stigmas linger.

And in an industry in which first-mover advantage matters greatly, community colleges were late to the party. Although the first community college, Joliet Junior College, was formed at the turn of the twentieth century, most currently existing campuses were established in the 1960s. By that time, the status hierarchy was already well entrenched.

An Awkward Position

So community colleges have diffuse missions, low tuitions, little respect, and chronic funding challenges.

The job of the college administrator in this setting is to make none of that matter. The students need the best education they can get, and the country needs a citizenry and a workforce that can meet the challenges of the twenty-first century. That simply will not happen without an effective community college sector.

Wishing the constraints away won't get the job done, though. What follows in this book is a series of reflections, based mostly on experience, about ways to play a difficult hand well. My goal is to help prospective administrators understand the changes that need to be made in order to fulfill the mission.

I should clarify up front that the community colleges at which I have worked have been in the Northeast and have had tenured and unionized faculty. Neither is universal throughout the sector. Even in my corner of the country, the Community College of Vermont is run entirely without full-time faculty. That's a very different model than the one I've experienced, and it no doubt brings challenges of its own. And I've never worked in the California system, so some of its quirks—particularly the way it arranges its funding—are beyond my experience.

Despite record enrollments, community colleges are swimming upstream against some powerful cultural currents. Simply put, they're designed to serve and produce a middle class that the economy no longer seems to want. The major growth in jobs seems to be occurring at the very high end of the scale and at the very low end. "Middle skills" positions—those that require some education beyond high school but not necessarily a four-year degree—are projected to remain prominent, though their real wages have been declining for some time.

In my darker moments, I wonder if the community college model— education for everyone who wants it—is a relic of a bygone culture. The political climate of the last few decades has strongly favored privatization, wealth polarization, and the reduction of state services that don't involve police. (That's not just a snarky observation. California spends more on corrections than it does on public higher education. At some point, you get what you pay for.) Whenever the social good of an educated citizenry is reduced to the private good of employability, I cringe. It would certainly be possible to reduce community colleges to job training centers, as some people seem to wish to do. The gravitational pull in that direction is powerful. Every year we lose a little more funding for core operations, but the grant support for workforce training just keeps growing.

As with public libraries, there's something irreducibly utopian, and maybe even absurd, about the idea of making higher education available to anyone who wants it, locally, on the cheap. It's an audacious, remarkable accomplishment, and one that has drawn interest from around the world. I consider it one of America's signal contributions to world culture, a worthy addition to Gerald Early's holy trinity of the Constitution, jazz, and baseball (quoted in Burns, 1994).

But maintaining this amazing monument to hope in the midst of a new and much harsher political climate will require more than just managerial savvy. It will require separating the mission from any given manifestation of it, and being willing to change the latter in order to strengthen the former. Institutions are necessary, but they can get stuck in time and become self-defeating. And for those of us in the middle—who try to keep things moving forward, even as the winds shift—it will be ever more important to keep our eyes on the horizon.

Phase Shifts

Higher education in the United States is in a transitional phase, with all of the awkwardness and uncertainty that implies; and as publicly funded institutions, community colleges may be more vulnerable to the coming changes than others.

One way to look at the current dilemmas we face is as clashes between the assumptions of different eras, what I call the preindustrial, industrial, and postindustrial.

The Preindustrial Model

Many of the trappings of higher education date back to the Middle Ages and religious orders in the Catholic Church. Graduation robes and Latin seals are conspicuous, if somewhat ancillary, manifestations of that. The more fundamental manifestations are in the concept of the faculty role.

In the earliest colleges, the faculty were largely derived from the clergy, and for all practical purposes they were the college. The idea of education as a calling paralleled the idea of priesthood as a calling—some people were chosen; most were not. Those who were chosen had a special gift and were entitled to special deference. In return, the obligation on those who were called was to be faithful to the text, as interpreted by a community of peers.

That's not to say that disagreements never occurred—any historian of religion would have a good chuckle over that—or that nobody ever used the trappings of the office to fulfill other agendas. But even allowing for the friction that inevitably occurs in any human endeavor, the basic idea held that professors were special, that they alone constituted the college, and that within their realm of expertise, they were entitled to a certain deference.

In the United States, of course, the transplant of a medieval European institution wasn't entirely clean. The oldest universities could approximate the old form with some success, but much of the early growth of higher education here was unabashedly vocational. "Teachers colleges," many of which went on to become comprehensive four-year state colleges, started with the clear mission of training elementary and secondary school teachers. (The phrase "normal school" was the accepted term of art, and it still pops up from time to time. Normal, Illinois, takes its name from the old Illinois Normal School, which is now Illinois State University.) Other schools taught surveying, mechanical arts, and agriculture. The Morrill Act of 1862 codified vocational education into law, establishing federal support to establish universities to train workers in the "useful arts" (as opposed to "liberal arts") (Cohen and Brawer, 2008).

As higher education expanded in the twentieth century, though, many of the quirkier organizational forms started to fall away, and a new normal was established. The mélange of organizational forms across the country started to standardize, although, ironically enough, they started to standardize around a blend of the medieval European model and the nineteenth-century European model of the research university. (Historians of higher education generally accept Johns Hopkins University as the first of that kind in the United States.)

The combination of rapid growth, de facto standardization, and a premodern organizational form led to some important tensions. Tenure, for example, didn't become a standard expectation across higher education until the 1940s, when the American Association of University Professors (AAUP) staked out its position in response to a series of abuses in the previous decades. But the idea of tenure went back centuries, and the AAUP's goal, oddly enough, was to replicate the centuries-old idea of the "calling" across a standardized bureaucracy.

The Industrial Model

For a while, it sort of worked. Higher education in the United States expanded dramatically in the post–World War II era, and the expansion lasted until about 1970. The expansion had several causes. The GI Bill gave veterans a newfound source of tuition money, and the midcentury rash of wars supplied a steady stream of veterans. The Cold War led to serious concerns about possible Soviet military superiority, and the Soviets' successful launch of the Sputnik satellite in 1957 gave a new sense of urgency to the development of science and technology and therefore of scientists and engineers. The first round of baby boomers hit college age in the mid-1960s, and they needed places to go. Draft deferments during the Vietnam era added to college enrollments, too, as did the wave of coeducation. For a while, the wind was at higher education's back.

For a few decades, campuses popped up all over the country at an impressive rate, and each new campus had to fill its faculty. That meant a once-in-a-lifetime job market for new PhD's in the evergreen disciplines. (I use the term "evergreen" in contrast to the "seasonal" disciplines that come and go. Math and English are evergreens; sports management is seasonal.) A campus that opened in, say, 1968, had to hire an entire cohort of faculty and administrators all at once. With such rapid expansion, it didn't matter much that graduate education was based on a pyramid scheme model. (New PhD's were produced at much higher rates than existing ones were retiring or leaving, and incumbents liked it that way because prestige and money accrued to faculty in graduate programs.) Pyramid schemes work pretty well when the market is expanding rapidly. But by the early 1970s, the rate of new hiring slowed drastically.

Community colleges grew at an especially rapid clip in the 1960s, and there, the clash of organizational forms and expectations was particularly dramatic. Many community colleges grew originally out of high schools. Their early forms therefore drew heavily on high school models rather than collegiate ones. In high schools, the ideas of faculty "calling" and deference simply weren't as pronounced; it was commonplace for a principal or superintendent to wield power unilaterally and bluntly. Faculty loyalties were expected to attach more to the local institution and community than to their scholarly disciplines; for a long time, PhD's were rare birds on community college faculties.

As institutions matured, though, and as faculty came on board from graduate programs rather than from high schools, the contradictions between the high school form and the professional expectations of tenure and deference often came to a head. One response to that was a wave of faculty unionization in the 1970s, as faculty decided to use a twentieth-century industrial form to win the respect they weren't getting otherwise. The drive met with mixed success, generally doing well in the more union-friendly states and not at all well in the rest of the country.

The Postindustrial Phase

When the producers of a desired good have a monopoly on its production, they can exact all manner of "rents." As economists use the term, *rents* are premiums above the price someone or something could command in an open market. In most cases, rents are taken as money. But they can also be taken in other forms, such as job security above and beyond what anyone else can expect.

In the middle of the twentieth century, rents were frequently extracted by unions negotiating with near-monopolies. The UAW was able to negotiate unsustainably high wages for a time, because the big three automakers were flush with money as a result of a temporary near-monopoly on the market. Although the union congratulated itself on its brilliance, the real reason for its success was a favored market position; when that favored market position ceased to hold, so did the union's ability to extract monopoly rents. Now, new hires at car factories are on a permanently lower salary tier than those who came before them. The same is happening at many public colleges, typically in the form of higher percentages of salary that have to be contributed to health insurance and retirement plans for newer hires than for older ones. The salaries themselves haven't changed, but take-home pay has.

In the case of the auto industry, unanticipated foreign competition broke the domestic near-monopoly on the market and shifted market power from incumbent workers to consumers. In higher education, the rise of the for-profits is playing much the same role.

Regional accreditation was the twentieth-century mechanism for keeping unwanted competition out of the market. For a time, it was able to keep for-profit competition mostly at bay, consigning it only to those fringes of the market (truck driving, cosmetology, bartending) that existing colleges didn't want.

That monopoly has started to crack, however.

In the past few decades, public higher education has expanded far more slowly than it did in the 1960s. More than twice as many community college campuses were built in the 1960s alone than in the four-plus decades since. But demand for higher education has continued to climb. The gap between what the public side of higher ed can—or is willing to—provide and what prospective students want created an opening for for-profit providers. And the for-profit providers make academic decisions based less on what the faculty want than on what the student market wants.

The Higher Learning Commission of the North Central Association, the regional accreditor that covers much of the middle of the country, bestowed its blessing on a few for-profits that quickly became national. The University of Phoenix and DeVry have the same accreditation as the University of Chicago and Northwestern. That accreditation allows them access to federal financial aid for students through Title IV, and they've taken full advantage of that access. The most recent statistics show that although the for-profits enroll about 12 percent of the undergraduates in the United States, they account for about 25 percent of the federal financial aid money (Nocera, 2011).

DIFFERENCES ON THE GROUND Although for-profits aren't all the same, as a sector, they generally focus much more on the students than on the faculty. I've never seen a for-profit with a tenure system, for example. The for-profits sell themselves—often quite aggressively—as student centered, with majors chosen for prospective employability and calendars built for student convenience. For example, when I worked at FPU, the teaching calendar was twelve months per year. Faculty had to teach twelve months per year as a condition of employment. The selling point to the students was that they could complete eight semesters in slightly less than three years, as opposed to the traditional four; as a result, they could start postgraduation employment sooner and reduce the opportunity cost of the degree. Even within the institutions themselves, the faculty were considerably less central than they are in most traditional colleges. The admissions staff was dramatically larger on a per-student basis than you usually see elsewhere, for example, and the career services office carried real political weight. The faculty mattered, but they were one group among others. And when someone fell down on the job, he or she could be removed.

Contrary to stereotype, FPU actually had full-time faculty who lasted there for decades. But they didn't last that long merely because they couldn't be touched; they lasted that long because they kept proving their value.

That's not to say that every decision made at FPU was wise or that every measure used made sense. In my time in administration there, I fought a series of losing battles to try to replace what I considered stupidly reductive measures with more valid ones. Eventually I got tired of trying to get the institution to think about the long term, and I left. Any institution can be run well or badly, and this one took what I considered a series of wrong turns.

Still, the culture shock I experienced upon arriving at the tenured and unionized community college was severe. It was one thing to have the chance to make a decision and get it wrong; it was something else altogether to find out that certain decisions simply couldn't be made because someone who had been granted impunity thirty years earlier would pitch a fit if we did. Suddenly the key question shifted from "What do the students need?" to "What will the faculty accept?"

Unsurprisingly, a great many curricular decisions were made based on the personal preferences of the faculty, rather than on any particular student need. For example, I saw this clearly with the physical education requirement at my first community college. Nobody could show that the students needed it, and in fact, many adult and part-time students resented it severely. But the long-tenured chair of the physical education department was a tenacious political infighter, and nobody wanted to deal with him. As a result, the requirement lasted far beyond anybody's recollection of the arguments in its favor. In fact, a local myth developed to the effect that it was some sort of statewide mandate.

I learned by accident that it wasn't. In working with some faculty to develop a proposal for a new major, we put together a proposed course of study that included all the required general education courses, and it kept coming in three credits too high. (The state set a hard cap on the number of credits that could be required for an associate's degree.) Going over the list repeatedly, the math was right; there were three credits too many. In frustration, I actually hunted down the state guidelines for gen ed requirements and cross-referenced them, only to discover that phys ed was the outlier. Despite local belief, phys ed simply was not required by the state.

When I brought that finding to the curriculum committee, the hostility was immediate and personal. What the hell did I think I was doing? Didn't I understand that Prof. X needed this job? If we approved a major without phys ed, soon other majors would go that way, too! What was I thinking?

Nearly nobody argued that students actually needed it. (The closest I heard to that was the chair of the English department, a personal friend of the phys ed chair, intoning sagely, "healthy body, healthy mind." I nearly fell off my chair.) The entire reference set for the discussion was internal.

Eventually, I won the argument, and the new program was adopted over the strenuous objections of the physical education chair, who retired the following year. Had he not been so close to retiring, I don't know that I would have prevailed.

DIFFERENCES IN THE CLASSROOM In my dean's role, I had observed classes at FPU and the community college. The difference in pedagogical styles was striking. At FPU, there had been incessant attention paid to ways to reach hard-to-reach students. Straight lecture was frowned on, and faculty were encouraged—sometimes almost pushed—to use both technology and group work to engage students. Some did it well, some did it less well, and some honored it in the breach, but the idea was clearly present that it was the professor's job to reach the students. Every professor was observed every year, and every raise was merit based.

At the community college, tenured professors were observed once every five years. Raises were contractual and across the board, with no merit component at all. (There was a significant seniority component, however.) Classes were taught almost exclusively in the teacher-centered lecture format. I felt as though I had gone back in time, and in a way, I had. Some of the lectures were quite good, of course, and some weren't, but most of them could easily have been delivered unchanged thirty years earlier. The most popular professor there used to answer his own yes-no questions in the course of his lectures; students dutifully copied them down for the multiple-choice tests that invariably followed.

Admittedly, I went directly from one extreme to the other, so the contrast was particularly striking. But each style made sense in its own context. When the whole point of the enterprise is to place students in jobs, then you judge faculty by how well they empower students. When the whole point of the place is to maintain jobs for people who got tenure three decades earlier, you avoid stirring the pot whenever you can. But I'm increasingly convinced that given the presence of a student-centered model, the teacher-centered model will have a hard time justifying itself, and rightly so.

When I raised doubts about the teacher-centered model, the responses I got from faculty were usually along the lines of "We uphold high standards and academic integrity." It's one of those phrases that sounds good but that actually functions to defeat critical thought. What, exactly, does upholding high standards mean? One could argue that it means doing things as they've always been done and letting the cream float to the top. Alternately, one could argue that it means making deliberate efforts to strengthen the students so that they can reach the higher standard.

"Integrity" is even more loaded. In my mind, academic integrity is the opposite of plagiarism. But in this context, it was used much more broadly to attack anything new or different. The integrity that was being preserved was the integrity of the past, taken as a whole. The most committed senior faculty seemed to think of themselves not as teachers but as docents.

From Time to Space

The technological shifts of the postindustrial period have also raised some basic questions for community colleges as geographically defined institutions. The taken-for-granted idea of one college per community is harder to maintain when the Internet allows students to cross state or national boundaries to take classes. Yet the governing (and taxing) authorities remain defined by geography. The sudden mismatch between politics and technology brings with it a distinctive set of challenges and opportunities.

Boundary Issues

Part of the historic mission of community colleges is implied in the name "community." Most community colleges draw almost entirely from a fairly well defined geographical region. In some states those regions are legally defined, whether as counties or districts; in others they're informal, but with very clear clustering on the ground.

Because most community colleges don't have dorms or other student housing, they have tended to draw students who live within commuting distance of campus. For most Americans, commuting distance limits their choices of community colleges to one or two. Funding models are mostly based on geography, with state or local funding combining with state or local tuition discounts. The idea is that local taxpayers have already contributed through their taxes, so they deserve a tuition break. (See Chapter Two for more on the ramifications of this arrangement.)

Undocumented students throw the entire "local discount" model into chaos. The premise of the local discount model is that we can distinguish local residents from outsiders, and charge accordingly. But what do you do when the "outsider" came into the country as a child and attended (and graduated from) a local public school?

One argument is that undocumented students are illegal by definition and therefore should not receive public subsidies such as public higher education. The K–12 system has to take all comers, but colleges don't. An undocumented student who completes a program and graduates still won't be able to work legally in this country, the argument goes, so what's the point?

This position isn't without a certain merit, though it strikes me as deeply problematic. It effectively punishes children for the sins of their parents, which offends any reasonable sense of justice. It creates a class of the permanently underemployable and undereducated, which is both morally suspect and politically dangerous. And it relies on a federal immigration system that could best be described as confused, if not byzantine.

The usual counterargument is that community colleges exist to serve everybody in the community; if undocumented people are in the community, the fact that they're here should be dispositive. After all, undocumented people pay property taxes (directly or indirectly), sales tax, and even income tax. Besides, if they're already in the K–12 system, why erect a stop sign at college?

This argument has the virtue of humanitarianism, but it isn't without its own shortfalls. For one, there's the basic fact that tearing down the stop sign at college doesn't tear down the stop sign at postcollege (or with-college) employment. Opening the doors to community college doesn't resolve the issue; it just postpones it.

There's also a basic equity issue in regard to people from neighboring counties or districts. When a kid from ten miles away has to pay double or triple tuition to attend the college of his choice because of where the county line falls, but the kid from Guatemala gets the local discount, you have a combustible political situation. I've had that conversation with an angry parent from one town over the county line; it isn't pretty.

From time to time, a brave legislator will reintroduce the DREAM act in Congress. The DREAM act would confer citizenship upon people who came over the border as children, once they've either graduated college or served a set amount of time in the military. The idea is to use a college degree or an honorable discharge as a "get out of jail free" card. From the perspective of a community college administrator, the DREAM act settles one part of the question nicely. It would probably lead to an enrollment boom, as undocumented young high school grads pursue education as a route to both citizenship and employability. But the DREAM act continually fails, falling prey to conflicted political attitudes on immigration.

The World Wide Classroom

Online education poses a challenge to the geographical model of community college systems, but it raises a host of other issues as well: economic, instructional, and administrative.

When colleges operated exclusively face-to-face, the geographical model was mostly self-enforcing. In the absence of dorms, most students had to be within easy driving distance. Some students would cross county lines for a particular program or to follow friends, but there was typically a limit to how far they would go.

But a student taking an online class could be anywhere with Internet access. At my college, we've recently had students from as far away as Kuwait and Thailand. Suddenly, counting on driving distance to resolve issues of differential tuition doesn't work.

To some degree, of course, that's positive. We have active-duty service members stationed in Afghanistan taking classes with us. (They get the local tuition rate.) That would have been impossible twenty years ago. Online education allows students with disabilities much greater access than in the past, and it works well with students whose personal life or work schedules make regular class attendance an issue. For example, adults with children often find online education ideal, as they can be home with the kids when they need to and can go online when the kids are in bed.

But when a community college from Pennsylvania is competing with another from Indiana and another from Tennessee for the "business" of a student in Texas, what does "community" mean?

We're only just beginning to confront this question in a serious way. So far, the overwhelming majority of students who take online classes at my college are also taking on-site classes; they use the convenience of online classes to make their schedules more flexible. (We expect that to change over time, but it has been the case so far.)

Flexibility applies to both the students and the institution. From the college's perspective, online classes are appealing in several ways.

For one, their flexibility allows, at least potentially, for a broader curriculum. In the face-to-face model, having thirty students across the college who want to take a particular class doesn't necessarily mean it can run, because there may not be a single time slot on which more than ten of them can agree. But with an online class, time conflicts suddenly become moot. If most students are comfortable with the technology, it becomes easier to aggregate a group of critical mass across varying schedules; suddenly the class that couldn't run, can.

Online classes also bring much lower infrastructure costs. During the enrollment boom of 2009, every physical classroom on campus was full during the morning and early afternoon. We simply could not add physical capacity during those hours. (We added some in the later afternoon, with good results, but some students had family or work conflicts that made that option impossible.) Adding physical classrooms is slow, difficult, and shockingly expensive. A smallish classroom building will quickly run to the $10–$20 million range, assuming no extraordinary facilities or conservation and geography issues. It will have to go out to bid—no quick process—and probably take at least two years of actual construction. It will require heat, water, and electricity, and will strain existing campus parking lots.

By contrast, adding server space is quick, cheap, and easy. Servers are getting more powerful and cheaper every year. You can easily add the capacity for a raft of new courses for $10,000 to $50,000, and get it up and running in a few weeks. It will consume a little electricity, but ongoing utility costs will be nominal and nothing approaching what a new building would consume. And online students don't need parking.

One place you won't find meaningful savings with online classes is the cost of instruction. Online education done well is labor intensive; if you want student learning outcomes and course completion rates to parallel those of on-site classes, you can't just stuff the sections with double or triple the number of students. If on-site English comp classes are capped at, say, twenty-two, then you'd be ill-advised to cap the online ones any higher than that. Successful online instructors regularly report that although their time is less structured, it adds up to more. (It's like the old joke about writing a dissertation—you can work any sixty hours a week you want.) The savings from online education are infrastructural, not instructional.

Still, some of the savings from online instruction have been realized because the added sections have largely been able to piggyback on previously existing services. At my college, for example, we pay for students to have access to an online tutoring service for targeted courses (like math), but most of the other student services are either unavailable online or irrelevant to it. And as long as most online students have been on-site students just filling out their schedules, that has worked tolerably well.

With the prospect of more students attending entirely online, though, the picture changes. Accrediting bodies require that students who attend entirely online get comparable services to students who come to campus. As the number of students who attend entirely online and live too far away to transact business on campus grows, colleges are forced to develop parallel processes for registration, library support, counseling, and the like.

As online enrollments grow, colleges frequently find that the relatively labor intensive workarounds for registration, academic advising, drop/add, and the like quickly become unsustainable. At that point, some of the savings from online instruction have to be reabsorbed in reinventing internal college processes, adding staff at odd hours, and upgrading both the back-office software and the technical skills of the service staff. When online classes were profitable sidelines, the basics of "how things get done" weren't significant issues, but as these classes become more central, at least some of the college infrastructure will have to change.

Many colleges have tried to adapt by moving piecemeal, through "hybrid" or "brick and click" courses. (I've even heard them called "surf and turf.") These courses feature some classroom instruction, but not as much as one would usually expect for the credit hours awarded; the difference is taken online.

Oddly, and frustratingly, student buy-in for hybrid classes has been persistently low, even as educational research has shown that hybrid classes typically deliver better student outcomes than either purely on-site or purely online classes.

From an institutional perspective, hybrid classes are ideal. Assuming, say, a fifty-fifty split between on-site and online delivery in a hybrid class, you could theoretically double the physical capacity of your campus without building anything. (If a Tuesday-Thursday class meets only on Tuesdays, with the Thursday part moved online, then you've picked up a classroom on Thursday. Suddenly you can fit two courses into one time slot.) They get around the difficulty of student identity verification—in the words of the old cartoon, on the Internet, nobody knows you're a dog—and allow for easy proctoring of exams. They give a natural venue for group work, lab work, or presentations. They maintain some connection to campus, so you can expect students to show up on a regular basis; that comes in handy when you would rather they transacted some of their business in person. And to the extent that hybrid classes actually result in better learning outcomes than do traditional classes, the economies of hybrids are real economies; the college saves money while actually improving student learning.

Yet students avoid them like the plague, and have for years. In talking with students, advisers, and faculty, I get the sense that students perceive hybrid classes as neither fish nor fowl. If they commit to the regular time slot of a traditional class, they don't want to also have to commit to navigating the software of an online class. If they like the independence of online classes, they don't want to have to schlep to a classroom on a regular basis. I've had students tell me with disarming candor that they perceive hybrid classes as two classes in one and therefore more work.

The only hybrid classes I've seen work have been those in rigidly sequenced cohort programs, like criminal justice or nursing. It strikes me as a natural fit for many lab science classes, because you could move the lecture part of the class online while keeping the lab part in the lab. When those classes have waiting lists, it's possible to shoehorn students into hybrid sections because they'll take whatever is available.

The popular perception of online education is badly out of sync with the reality of it. Online education and for-profit education are sometimes discussed as if they were the same thing. It's true that the for-profits have been quick to move online, but they haven't been alone, and they haven't entirely abandoned the traditional classroom, either. "Online" refers to a delivery style rather than a motive.

I expect that perceptions will shift over time as students vote with their virtual feet. But in the meantime, administrators have an uphill battle in trying to explain the nuances of delivery to a public that's trapped in some older stereotypes. And the question of how to reconcile an institution that's increasingly divorced from geography with a taxation system that's resolutely place bound remains unclear.

Looking into the Future

In recognition of the very real challenges to the old geographical "service area" idea that new technologies pose, I hope to see community colleges work less as independent actors and more as statewide or even regional systems. Does every program need to run at every campus? Right now, "consortial" agreements between campuses in which multiple campuses share an individual program are unsustainably labor intensive, and they tend to fall apart quickly. But allocating specialized programs by region offers to keep implementation sustainably clean and simple, while still allowing students access to the programs they want. Such an arrangement could also allow for cost savings on each campus, as each wouldn't need to dedicate scarce square footage to single-purpose labs.

Of course, the greatest challenges—both short term and long term—are financial. The next chapter addresses those directly.

FUNDING

WHERE THE MONEY COMES FROM, WHERE
IT GOES, AND WHY THERE'S NEVER ENOUGH

ACADEMIC ADMINISTRATORS ARE CAUGHT BETWEEN TWO POINTS OF VIEW:

Why the hell does tuition go up so fast? Where's the market discipline? Who do these people think they are?

Why the hell are they replacing full-time faculty with adjuncts? Where's the respect for quality? Who do these people think they are?

In these questions—all of which are legitimate—administrators are mostly the "these people" taking the blame. This chapter is my attempt to explain the double-bind in which many administrators and colleges find themselves, and how it came to pass. I address the constraints administrators face when making budgetary decisions and some of the unintended consequences of those decisions. I also suggest that the pressures are likely to get worse before they get better, so incoming leaders would be well advised not just to wait for the budgets of the 1960s to come back.

First, let me clarify that at any given college, several variables are in play simultaneously:

Operating budget. This is the money that covers ongoing costs: salaries and benefits, consumable supplies (those with shelf lives of less than a few years—everything from lab chemicals to toner cartridges), small equipment purchases, utility payments, direct financial aid to students, and maintenance of buildings and equipment.

Capital budget. This is the money that covers long-term physical plant costs. Construction and renovation of buildings, major equipment or land purchases, and various new facilities (gyms, stadiums, and so on) are covered here. Computers are usually also accounted for here.

Grants. Most community colleges have at least some grant-funded activity, and the more active ones have a surprising amount. Grants can be public (government funded) or private, and each grant has its own requirements for reporting, supervision, and spending. Many of them have requirements for "sustainability," or absorption by the college, after the expiration date of the grant; knowing that, leaders need to choose carefully which grants to pursue.

Contracts and continuing education. Although this is invisible to many faculty, community colleges often draw significant income from their noncredit and contract offerings. Noncredit offerings have considerable range. One flavor is the basic personal enrichment class: pottery, say, or engine repair. A second is adult basic education—adult literacy, English as a Second Language (ESL) or English for Speakers of Other Languages (ESOL), and GED prep. Finally, many colleges offer "workforce development" courses for a profit. These classes—for example, workshops in new software packages or grant writing—teach short-term job-related skills.

Federal and state financial aid. Although this money finds its way into the operating budget, it's indirect, as it goes to the student and then to the institution. However, the institution is responsible for monitoring, verifying, and tracking; for all practical purposes, it's also responsible for shepherding the student through the process.

Foundations. An increasing number of community colleges have foundations to coordinate philanthropic giving. Typically, foundation money is used primarily for student scholarships. However, some colleges also use some of it to pay for selected equipment purchases or dedicated campus offices, like Centers for Teaching Excellence or specialized science labs. This is also where colleges solicit donations for naming rights of buildings and campus facilities.

Reserves and endowments. Although community colleges don't usually have endowments, many of them have reserves. Reserves are usually intended to serve as rainy-day funds, and they're often accrued through small operating surpluses in good years.

The boundary lines between these various categories aren't always clear or obvious. A donor to the foundation may think of herself as giving a grant, for example. I've seen software considered "operating," and I've seen it considered "capital." It's not always clear where maintenance stops and renovation starts. However, even while acknowledging some fuzziness around the edges, it's worth keeping these categories straight. That's because (with rare exceptions) administrators aren't free to mix them.

Let's look at each of these categories, and their associated consequences, in greater depth.

Operating Budgets

When people talk about budgets, they usually mean operating budgets. In most colleges, the vast majority of the operating budget is devoted to labor. Over time, that has difficult consequences for cost control.

The Productivity Problem

Economists define *productivity* as the value of goods or services that can be produced in a given amount of time. Call it dollars per hour, to keep things simple.

Over the last century, in the economy as a whole, productivity has gone up anywhere from 1 to 4 percent a year (Gordon, 2010). Economists generally agree that increased productivity makes sustained prosperity possible. It doesn't assure prosperity by itself—the gains from improved productivity could be hoarded entirely by a small sliver of the population, say—but it's a precondition. Without sustained increases in productivity over time, there will be stagnation or decline. And if the economy as a whole becomes more productive but a given sector doesn't, then that sector will grow inexorably more expensive relative to other things.

In manufacturing, productivity gains are usually the result of technological innovations. The assembly line made it possible for the same number of workers to produce far more cars per hour, driving down their cost. Information technology has revolutionized logistics, making global supply chains (and big-box discount retail) possible. These industries have certainly created some fabulously wealthy people, and they've also reduced costs for most of us.

In services, productivity gains can be harder to generate. Medical care has seen its share of technological advances, but we've mostly used those advances to improve outcomes rather than to decrease costs. That's a perfectly defensible choice—what better to spend money on than life itself?—but it doesn't come cheap. It's hard to speed up one-on-one visits, especially when each case is unique.

Education as currently structured falls into a similar trap. We measure degrees by the time it's supposed to take to get them: two-year degrees, four-year degrees, and so on. We charge students by the credit hour or the course, and we set minimum numbers of credit hours or courses to get a degree. In other words, we set the time-to-degree ratio as a constant. A three-credit class requires forty-five hours of seat time, just as it did forty years ago. Despite all the money spent on educational research, educational technology, alternative assessment, and the like, a three-credit class takes just as long as it ever did. In economic terms, the net productivity increase has been zero for a very long time.[1]

This means that the only way to keep up with the productivity gains in the rest of the economy has been to raise prices. If you can't produce more, you can just charge more, as long as the demand is still there.

Seen in this light, the apparent contradiction between paying less for faculty and charging students more isn't contradictory at all. They're two versions of the same thing: attempting to wring greater productivity out of an unchanging activity. (The third common strategy, of course, is larger class sizes—more tuitions per hour.)

Health care and higher education are the only two industries I know in which technology is routinely added to the production process without concern for whether or not it improves economic productivity. Not coincidentally, health care and higher education are the two industries whose costs have outstripped general inflation for several decades running. In health care, new technologies are adopted because they're expected to lead to medically positive outcomes, even if those outcomes are incredibly expensive.[2]

Colleges adopt technologies for a similar reason—not because they save the institution money or increase productivity, but because the industries for which they prepare students adopt them. When the photography and graphics industries went digital, our programs in photography and graphics had to make the change too. As nurses in many clinical settings are switching from clipboards to mobile tablet computers, our nursing program has had to purchase the same technology to keep up. We've had to install Wi-Fi across campus simply to keep up with student (and transfer school, and employer) expectations. The typical private sector company will invest in technology only if it sees a payoff for itself. We invest in technology to keep current with the expectations of others, even when it's a substantial, ongoing deadweight cost for us.

(Although it's not often appreciated on the outside, the political push to get community colleges more tightly focused on workforce development will certainly increase the cost of instruction even more. Employers who have discovered that they can outsource their training costs to the public sector would be foolish not to do so; if they don't, their competition will. A serious examination of college costs needs to include a discussion of the increasingly expensive favors colleges are doing for private employers by absorbing the costs that employers once covered for themselves.)

The increasing importance of technology has led to much larger IT staffs on campus over time. Because the IT staff doesn't teach, its positions and costs are usually lumped under "administration," as if they were somehow supervisory. The resulting budgetary bulge leads to some distorted debates on campus, as faculty advocates rage against "administrative bloat" without realizing that they're really seeing a category error.

Rising expectations of colleges in nontechnical areas have also driven costs higher. For example, when most community colleges were built in the 1960s, they did not have Offices for Students with Disabilities. In the wake of the passage of the Americans with Disabilities Act in 1990, most colleges do now, usually involving multiple employees and all manner of costly assistive technology. Counseling offices and academic advising offices have flourished, as colleges have tried to address student attrition and mental health issues.

Dual-enrollment programs and "college transition" programs have also multiplied over the years. These programs offer high school–age students academic credit at both the high school and the college level for a given class. Although there have always been occasional prodigies taking the stray advanced math class, these programs are different in both scale and purpose. They draw on a much wider range of students—sometimes average students, sometimes even students identified as high risks for dropping out, and, in much of the country, a significant cohort of homeschoolers. Each dual-enrollment program brings with it its own managers, whose job it is to finesse the logistical, legal, and academic differences between high schools and the community college.

When Tailwinds Became Headwinds

For a while, colleges were able to get away with price increases with relatively little resistance. In the public sector, a booming economy in the 1960s allowed for booming public subsidies, so the direct cost to students remained deceptively low. (Although it's hard to imagine now, tuition at City University of New York remained zero into the early 1970s.) Even once tuition started climbing, federal and state financial aid initially absorbed a good chunk of it, so the real cost to middle-class students was still quite low. And the shifts in employment patterns in the broader economy increased the relative value of a college degree, so even as the degree became more expensive, the return on investment was still high enough to make it worthwhile.

By the 2000s, though, the various fig leaves started falling away. Student loans became a progressively larger percentage of financial aid, often with severe financial consequences for young graduates in their first few years in the workforce. Consecutive cycles of jobless recoveries and steadily more severe recessions led to a paucity of well-paying jobs for new grads just as their student loan payments set new records.

And the political willingness to carry the brunt of the cost of public higher education had faded much earlier, as the anti-tax backlash of the 1980s became the conservative juggernaut of subsequent decades. State subsides became much smaller proportions of college budgets, with the balance shifted mostly to students. Even if a college kept its overall spending in relative check, tuition still went up quickly to compensate for the lost ground on the legislative subsidy side. State budgets had to fund multiple labor-intensive service operations—corrections, health care, K–12—that didn't have alternative revenue streams on which to rely. Because higher ed has an alternative revenue stream, it has been forced to rely on it ever more heavily.

Capital Budgets

The administration is pleading poverty on salaries, but it's spending millions on a new building! Where are its priorities?

In my first few years of administration, it slowly dawned on me that it's easier to get a new building built than it is to pay people to work in it. That's because the sources of money are different, and the different funding streams can't be mixed.

In some states, the buildings are the actual property of the state and are paid for by the state. In others, the buildings belong to the college, but the state puts up "matching" money in exchange for compliance with its sense of what ought to be done. In an increasing number of cases, a major donor comes along at the end and buys the naming rights. (It's much less common for the donor to actually pay for the construction before or during the process.) The funds for that matching money are earmarked specifically for construction and cannot be reallocated by the college for anything else. (In the wake of the Great Recession, there's a new trend for states to have colleges borrow money themselves for construction and renovation projects, even while the states maintain control of the buildings [Kiley, 2012].)

Construction is usually considered a form of economic development and a major political plum. Politicians love to cut ribbons, and the public likes results it can see. A nifty new technology center on campus will get good press, make great copy for various campus publications, and provide an immediate and tangible improvement in the campus experience of some students. It will also arrive with shiny new systems for everything— "green" heating and cooling systems, the latest technology, LEED certification, full ADA compliance, and no wear and tear.

Having been through the drill a few times now, though, I can attest that it isn't quite that simple.

The True Costs of Construction

New space will inevitably set off a scramble on campus, as incumbent offices jockey for the most desirable newly vacated places. If the new space is the result of a renovation rather than entirely new construction, the space scramble will occur twice: first as the existing area is emptied out and the former occupants are moved into "swing space," and again when they move back in and the "swing space" goes up for grabs. (If those moves involve people changing the parking lots they use, you can expect serious angst among those whose parking lot was invaded.) Although renovations are usually cheaper than new construction, they're considerably messier. They're much harder to plan and often much less satisfying, as the results are constrained by legacy choices.

Renovation or construction can often be funded (in whole or in part) externally, but maintenance of what has been built has to be funded internally through the operating budget. Savvy managers know that, and will negotiate to have the cost of extended warranties for certain items folded into the initial cost, the better to defer the onset of new liabilities.

Because capital and operating funds come from different sources, it's not unusual for a college that has access to a hefty pot of capital to still have to scrimp on operating expenses. If a college accepts $5 million from the state to pay for half of the cost of a new building, then it isn't on the hook only for the other $5 million. It's also on the hook for the increased maintenance and utility costs that the new facility will inevitably incur. It's theoretically possible to account for those costs in advance, but in practice, operating budgets are too volatile for that. Instead, the usual consequence is a new round of maintenance triage, in which the college decides—passively or actively—which items to defer and which to pursue.

"Deferred maintenance" has become so normal that it's an actual budget line at many places. Like "professional development," it's one of the first places to go when there's an operating shortfall. Yes, we should upgrade the lighting in Q lot, but does it have to be done right now? Yes, the boiler in the administration building is wheezing, but do you think it could limp through another couple of years? Because resources are scarce and emergencies can happen at any time—in my observation, they almost always involve water—matters that are annoying rather than dangerous can go unaddressed for years. Some cynical administrations will inflate the figures for deferred maintenance as a tactic in collective bargaining, using it to parry union claims of plenty of loose money lying around. I'm no fan of this strategy, not least because it contributes to the unhelpful confusion between capital spending and salary budgets, but it happens.

Decisions to defer maintenance are individually rational but cumulatively devastating. Neglecting a small leak in the summer leads to ice getting in there in the winter, making the leak bigger. When the ice melts, especially if it's in the context of a hard rain combined with an abrupt snow melt, now you have indoor flooding, which leads to carpet degradation, mold, and fried electrical equipment. It would have been much cheaper to patch the leak when it first appeared.

I've seen colleges where some administrator long ago made the cynical calculation that it was best just to let deferred maintenance accumulate, and wait for the periodic pots of construction money to fall from the sky to replace the decaying older stuff altogether. And there are times when that can work. But if you time it wrong, you get a level of dinginess that's really beyond reasonable repair and that can last for years.[3]

Naming

The relationship between construction and philanthropy can be spotty. Donors like science labs, computer centers, theaters, and athletic facilities. They generally don't like parking lots, storage sheds, or administrative offices. (I've never seen a snowplow storage shed with a donor's name attached.) Parking is where the gap between available funding and on-the-ground need is usually the greatest. I've never seen a college that didn't have a parking problem, and I've never seen a parking lot project given a high priority. Announce that you're adding a new building that will allow you to add a thousand students, and bathe in the praise. Announce a parking lot to go with it, and prepare for battle.

Parking lots galvanize all manner of opposition. Environmentalists who don't get upset about new buildings will go ballistic about new parking lots. They see lots as symbolic concessions to automobile culture, which is the source of tremendous environmental damage. To my mind, that's half true. Yes, automobile culture leads to tremendous environmental and quality-of-life damage. But parking lots aren't symbolic concessions to it. They're real, and necessary, concessions to it. As environmentally damaging as a thousand new cars on campus would be—and I don't dispute the point—a thousand new cars slowly circling full parking lots looking for spaces would be that much worse. In the absence of viable alternatives to cars for most people, and in the absence of dorms on campus, most students (and faculty and staff) will drive. It's a cost of doing business. Failing to account for the cost doesn't make it go away. If anything, it raises the cost insidiously by creating emergencies where they didn't have to exist.

Alternative Strategies for Increasing Capacity

Because physical plant is a major cost item, and most of its cost is incurred whether it's used a little or a lot, there's a compelling economic argument for using it to the hilt. Whenever the college is paying to heat an entire building, any empty classrooms represent lost revenue opportunities.

As with restaurants or theaters, though, there's usually a predictable temporal rhythm of demand. A restaurant owner knows the place will be packed at 7:00 PM and nearly empty at 4:00, so she makes the calculation that an early bird special is better than nothing, even if the unit profit is lower. A theater owner makes the same calculation with a bargain matinee.

In the case of community colleges, there are typically two peaks. The first and bigger one is from about 9:00 AM to about 2:00 PM Monday through Thursday. (On campus, we call this "prime time.") During prime time, nearly every classroom and parking space is taken, and the place is hopping. It dies down quickly after that, though, becoming almost desolate by 3:00. It fills up again, if to a lesser extreme, at around 6:00.

I mention this because it sheds light on the issue of capacity. For example, in 2009, my college experienced a double-digit percentage enrollment increase in a single year, even though it was already operating at over 90 percent capacity during prime time, and it didn't add any new buildings. How did we do it? By realizing that capacity is a function of both space and time. The relevant question isn't "Where did all the new students go?" but "When did all the new students go?" We couldn't add meaningful numbers at noon, but we could (and did) add a host of new sections at 4:00. Classrooms that had previously lain fallow in the late afternoon, consuming heat without generating revenue, were pressed into service.

Because we had to heat them anyway, the economic argument was clear. And many students were motivated enough (or available enough) to actually take the 4:00 classes.

As I mentioned in the previous chapter, space crunches are also part of the appeal, from the administrative perspective, of online classes. Because online classes don't need classrooms, you can add them without building anything. Adding server space is far cheaper than adding classroom space. When classroom space is scarce, this advantage is not to be ignored. Unfortunately, because online pedagogy is still relatively new and largely foreign to the experience of many senior faculty, online offerings are still often a function of faculty willingness to do them. And "early adopters" aren't always where you want them to be, which means that online offerings are frequently "lumpy" by department. Many of the potential logistical gains of online education have yet to be realized, because the courses that haven't gone online yet fall under the local purview of faculty who won't—for whatever reason—do online instruction.

Technically, of course, this shouldn't be an issue. Scheduling belongs to management, not to faculty, and it is a management right to schedule an online class. Although faculty often wield claims of "academic freedom" as a club to beat into submission anything they don't like, academic freedom does not give individual professors veto power over entire curricula. This element of academic freedom—deciding what shall be taught—rests with the college as an institution, not with faculty as individuals.

But on the ground, that distinction doesn't always apply. Yes, it would be theoretically possible to hire a new adjunct to teach an online class over the objections of the regular faculty. But in practice, getting other things done requires a level of sustained cooperation that makes the occasional scorched-earth maneuver untenable. Yes, it's annoying that a single department can unilaterally tank an entire series of online degree programs by pitching a collective fit about labs. But doing the academic equivalent of declaring eminent domain to allow the information highway to go through would do untold damage to any number of other programs. It's the bane of the administrator's existence to reward tantrums, but reality dictates that some battles simply aren't worth the cost. If possible, you're much better off making the desired option more attractive—whether by creative exposure or direct incentive—than trying to coerce acceptance.

Space shortages aren't just a function of overall demand. They're also the unintended fallout of customization. Capacity can be limited by specialization. A well-equipped biology lab would be a poor choice for an English class and a catastrophic one for the jazz ensemble. As community colleges try to be "responsive" to community need by adding occupation-specific programs, there's a tendency for general-purpose classrooms to be consumed and converted into special-purpose labs. Over time, those specialized facilities take on lives of their own.

On my campus, for example, we have a crime-scene lab for the criminal justice program, an astronomy lab, a robotics lab, a teaching kitchen, photography darkrooms, graphic design labs, a human patient simulator lab, several biology and chemistry labs, music practice rooms, art studios, engineering labs, and a radiology lab, just for starters. None of those can be easily or sensibly repurposed on a piecemeal basis. Once you've outfitted a room for a single purpose, it's pretty much restricted to that purpose.

In the absence of new construction, this means that new programs in occupational fields will tend to crowd out general-purpose classrooms. This, too, is part of the appeal of online courses to administrators. If you can convert the regular classroom into a dedicated lab and then move the previous occupants online, then you've doubled your capacity without building anything, assuming that your faculty and students are willing to move online as needed.

Revenue Sources: Silver Linings, Complete with Clouds

The obverse of costs, of course, is revenues. The revenue structure for community colleges is different than in the rest of higher education. Although the specifics vary by state and sometimes by campus, the general categories here tend to be common across the country.

State and Local Appropriations

Historically, states and localities have been the major funders of community colleges. The annual appropriations from states and localities were the single most important factor in keeping tuition and student fees low.

The balance between states and localities has varied across the country. Some states have county-based systems. (Depending on the state, sometimes community colleges are actually called county colleges.) In county-based systems, the state typically allots a certain amount of money for the county colleges, and each county supplements the appropriation for its own college. County funding can come out of general county funds, as in New Jersey, or from dedicated "millages," as in Michigan. (A millage is a dedicated property tax, often set by referendum.) Typically, county-based systems charge premium tuition for students from outside the county, on the theory that county residents have already paid part of their share through local property taxes.

Other states leave localities out of the picture, and centralize both control and funding. In Massachusetts, for example, county governments were dissolved in the early 2000s, and community colleges receive no local funding at all. California, characteristically, does a hybrid, with affluent areas sometimes supplementing state appropriations.

The theory behind public funding, whatever the state-local balance, is that an educated population is, at least in part, a public good. Public funds allow public colleges to charge students less than the full cost of the education they receive, thereby making higher education affordable and more likely to be used.

In most states, the dismal reality is that state funding has been declining as a percentage of college budgets for several decades, and the rate of decline is accelerating. The reasons for that go well beyond the scope of this book, but there's no obvious reason to expect a significant reversal of the trend in the foreseeable future. Administrators who keep waiting for the money fairy to visit and restore the levels of support that colleges received a generation ago are waiting in vain.

Frustratingly, though, states that have become much more modest in their funding support have adopted no such humility when it comes to passing mandates. States don't pay the piper like they once did, but they try to call the tune as never before.

Tuition and Fees

As state and local support has dwindled, tuition and fees have increased dramatically to make up much of the difference. Put differently, colleges have shifted much of the cost of education from the public as a whole to students as individuals. (As will be discussed, some of that cost finds its way back to the public in the form of financial aid.)

In most states, tuition is considered the all-purpose funding, and fees are dedicated to specific purposes. Tuition is usually the headline number, so it's becoming common for colleges to increase dedicated fees at higher rates than tuition in order to take the edge off the increases to the most conspicuous number.

And that's not always disinguous. Lab fees have long been assessed for lab sciences, for example, and studio fees are common for certain kinds of art classes. The idea behind those fees is that some classes are inherently far more expensive to run, whether because of facilities, consumables, or both, and that charging students a little extra to offset those costs is relatively fair because the students in those classes are the ones getting the benefits.

The distinction between tuition and fees can get squishy, though. A lab fee for a particular class is easy to explain, but a general "campus technology fee" looks a little more like tuition. (That's especially true when a college charges an online student the same "student activities fee" that it charges on-campus students.) Some states have held the line on tuition by pushing all increases into the fees category, which has the annoying side effect of making "free tuition" scholarships much less meaningful.

Decades of cost-shifting from state appropriations to tuition and fees have had the cumulative effect of making community college budgets much more enrollment driven than they once were. That may not matter much when enrollments are rising, but it makes a tremendous difference when they stagnate or fall. In the past, healthy state support could buffer a college through a down cycle in enrollment; now, the college has to make cuts when enrollments drop. The intersection of declining revenues with high fixed costs makes countercyclical investment—which is otherwise cheaper—much harder.

Until recently, community college administrators as a group were able to pay less attention to other sources of funding than have their counterparts in other sectors. But as states continue to cut, and students start to hit the limits of what they can pay, community college administrators will have to become more like their counterparts in the private college sector. Fundraising and grantsmanship will likely become progressively more important.

Grants

Grants can be public or private, though the vast majority at most community colleges are public.

Grants are gifts with strings: a set of rules that govern how the grant money can be spent. That can create issues when the assumptions behind the grant don't align well with local union contracts or state regulations. For example, the Gates foundation has endowed a set of programs under the "Gateway" banner. These programs are designed to increase retention and graduation rates among underrepresented populations. They work on an "intrusive advisement" model, in which a single "point person" is paid to coordinate a program for a given cohort of students, to advise those students, and to teach classes to those students. ("Intrusive advisement" differs from traditional advisement in that it recasts the adviser's role. The traditional adviser holds office hours, and students who want advice can show up as needed. The intrusive adviser chases students down and monitors their attendance and progress. To its fans, the intrusive advisement model is proactive and responsive. To its detractors, the adviser's role smacks of the old truant officer.) The idea is to give the students a single primary point of contact within the college, so that they'll be comfortable going to somebody if an issue arises.

Where there are strong unions, though, strict compliance with that structure is impossible. "Coordinators" are administration, and administrators can't teach. Professors can teach, but they can't manage. Harmonizing grant rules with local rules can be a nightmare and can even be altogether prohibitive. We've actually had to trim the staffing of grant-funded programs to be able to bring the salaries in line with the collective bargaining agreements, because the unions were able to make a legal case for getting those positions reclassified as unit (union) jobs. As a result, the program had to limit its reach.

Some grants, like Perkins, are ongoing.[4] They're renewable indefinitely and can become more or less part of your baseline operations. These grants are the most valuable by far. Because they stretch over years, they allow for long-term planning. They have strings of their own, of course; the academic advisers that my college pays for through the Perkins grant can work only with students in Perkins-approved majors, for example—but when the program sticks around for a long time, you can build the rest of your budget around those strings and do what needs to be done.

Most grants have expiration dates, though. Increasingly, they're intended as "seed money" for projects that the grantor hopes the college will absorb into its own budget after the grant expires. (The term for that is "sustainability.") Seed-money grants are supposed to get a program started, on the assumption that the college will keep it going after a few years. When a program graduates from grant funding to internal college funding, it's referred to as going from "soft money" (the grant) to "hard money" (the college).

Sustainability is a lovely goal, of course, but it brings issues of its own. At the most basic level, if an operation were sustainable without the grant, the college wouldn't need the grant. The whole point of going after grant money is that you don't have enough on your own to do what needs to be done.

Federal grants often have clauses prohibiting the use of grant money to "supplant" college money. This means that grant money is not to be used to pay for things the college would otherwise have paid for itself; it's only to be used for things that otherwise would not have been done. (The catchphrase is "supplement, not supplant.") The theory, as near as I can tell, is that grantors like to know that their money is making a difference, and it's difficult to make the case for making a difference when the money was used for routine expenses. The problem, though, is that with public funding in decline and with tight rules on supplanting in place, grant money is walled off from the areas of greatest need. It can pay for extras, but it can't pay for the core. Then when the grant expires, the college has to hollow out the core even more to meet the sustainability requirement for the supplement. When the core is being hollowed out, the rule goes from understandable to dysfunctional.

Predictability is an issue of its own. When state budgets gyrate unpredictably, and federal mandates come and go for reasons of their own, it's difficult for an administration to make a credible spending promise five years in the future. The college administration may well change hands by then, with the new administration having different priorities. The federal and state political winds will almost certainly shift, though it's hard to predict exactly in which direction. Even allowing for those, new needs will likely develop in that time, and they may or may not take greater importance in the future.

Some agencies—I won't name any names here—even like to delay payments of promised money, but then forbid "backfilling" once the money comes. Say, for example, that my college gets a grant to fund math tutors, but the money that's supposed to arrive in August is delayed until November. The college fronts the money for the tutors through November. Then the college is told that it can't recoup from the grant the money it has already paid those tutors; what it spent is simply gone. Repeat this a few times, and even a generous grant becomes far more expensive than it's worth; it has been turned into an unfunded mandate.

Of course, with any grant-funded initiative, there's the ever present but rarely discussed possibility of programmatic failure. Grants now usually come with a requirement that some sort of outcomes assessment be built in from the start. In some ways, that makes perfect sense; it's certainly helpful to know whether a gift had its intended effect or not. But there's a basic tension between the candor required to make a useful assessment and the successful outcomes required to get the grant renewed. If you receive a grant award to roll out developmental learning communities over five years with the goal of increasing student pass rates, and the pass rates don't improve, you can kiss the money good-bye at the end of the initial period. Savvy project managers have found ways to massage data to tell the stories they need told, but there again, the interest being served may not be the students'.

Whenever I attend meetings of the League for Innovation or the AACC, I'm struck by the ratio of papers on "Here's a project that worked!" to "Here's a project that didn't." It's typically about 100:0, as one doesn't advance one's career by owning failure. But honesty compels me to admit that most projects either fail, or succeed only in very limited ways. True breakthroughs are rare.

To my mind, the ideal grant would be semipermanent, targeted to helping us do things we either already do or should already be doing, and based on allowing experimentation. "Supplanting" would be a sign that the task was actually important. As with good teaching or good science, you need to accept some amount of error or disconfirmation as part of the learning process. Nobody gets it right every time, but you wouldn't know that from looking at grants.

Suggestion to funding agencies: one really productive but low-cost use of federal dollars would be to fund *comparative* studies of similar projects in different contexts. Pay people who don't work at Compass Direction State (CDS) to study how CDS tried to, say, improve graduation rates of underrepresented populations, then to compare what CDS did to what Private Catholic College did. Include failures, errors, and partial successes in the story. Until we can get past the conflict of interest that bedevils most discussion of grant-funded programs, we'll keep drowning in very expensive happy talk.

Contracts and Continuing Education

In many community colleges, the corporate, noncredit side of the house is separate from the academic, credit-granting side. The corporate, noncredit side is run for a profit, and the profits are used to subsidize the academic side. The two sides coexist somewhat uneasily, as they operate by very different rules and with very different assumptions, but they need each other. The noncredit side benefits from the name recognition and goodwill generated by the credit side, and the credit side simply could not function without the profits generated by the noncredit side.

The noncredit side runs several broad varieties of programming. The classic one, and the one with which most people are familiar, is the short-term personal enrichment course that is run for a profit. Because the courses don't carry academic credit, they can be of varying lengths and levels of rigor. This is the pottery class offered at night for whoever wants to take it. Depending on local interest and facilities, I've seen courses ranging from resume writing to line dancing to Chinese cooking.

These classes are often quite popular among retirees (although they draw people of all ages and stages of life), which offers a double benefit for the college: retirees who take these classes have resources, and they are often politically powerful beyond their numbers. If a college can build goodwill among the affluent retirees in the community, it will do well with the local legislators.

Although personal enrichment courses are perhaps the best-known noncredit offerings, most of the recent attention has gone to "workforce development" programs. In most cases, these are not traditional academic subjects. The idea behind workforce development is that employers need employees with certain skill sets, and workers need current and improving skill sets to get and keep good jobs; therefore, some money spent on training workers will more than pay off over time in higher employment rates, higher wages, and a higher tax base. When it works, it creates a virtuous circle: employers expand because they have the workers to do it; workers get trained because they see a payoff; the local economy thrives, which draws other companies and new jobs; welfare costs drop and tax revenues grow; and everybody wins.

Workforce development classes can run in several different ways. Sometimes the college simply runs classes along the personal enrichment model when it has a sense that a given skill is in high demand. For example, my college regularly runs classes in the Microsoft Office suite, Quick-Books, and other commonly used software packages. The courses fill with people who work in offices or who are trying to get jobs in offices.

Alternately, sometimes companies will contract with colleges to run courses specifically for their own employees. For example, a local branch of a well-known telecommunications company recently contracted with my college to run a training class on installing home electronics systems for its employees, and a local hospital regularly contracts with the college to run ESOL courses for its maintenance workers, to enable them to learn enough English to be more effective on the job. In these cases, sometimes the college will actually send an instructor to a sponsoring company's site to teach the class. Because the classes don't carry academic credit, they can be of varying lengths, depending on client preference and need.

Workforce development classes are also sometimes grant driven. For example, the Obama administration has sponsored grants for programs to prepare people to work in "green industries." The idea is to develop a skilled workforce in an area in which there seems to be general demand, in the hope that once a critical mass is there, the employment opportunities will emerge.

As with any exercise in picking winners, this approach is hit-and-miss. If the sponsoring agency guesses wrong, it's easy to wind up with people trained for jobs that don't exist, or that don't exist in numbers sufficient to absorb the graduates of the programs. (Anyone who got a doctorate in a liberal arts discipline over the last couple of decades knows how that works.) Early results of the green jobs programs suggest that it's dangerous to get too far ahead of market demand when setting up these programs.

Many colleges also offer adult basic education classes in the noncredit area. In the academic hierarchy, these classes are predevelopmental. They're intended primarily for recent immigrants or people whose high school education was either truncated or entirely unsuccessful. They are usually grant funded, and nearly always have long waiting lists. Adult basic education covers basic literacy and math, and very low-level English courses for people whose first language is something else. It also includes GED prep programs. The material in these courses doesn't even rise to the level of developmental classes, but it's tremendously important in daily life. Simply learning enough English to get a low-skill job can make a world of difference in the life of someone on the margins. Adult basic ed typically loses money, but it's at the core of the community service mission of the community college.

Dual- (or concurrent-) enrollment and college-transition programs bridge the noncredit and credit-bearing areas and are becoming increasingly popular. The Gateway to College program mentioned earlier, sponsored by the Bill and Melinda Gates Foundation, is a conspicuous example. Programs like these typically target at-risk high school populations and build interventions to prevent them from walking away from education altogether. Frequently the model involves teaching college classes to high school–age students and awarding them both high school and college credit. The appeal is supposed to be that it gets the students away from the dysfunctional high school setting and into a college setting, with the goal of making college seem real to them.

With any program targeting at-risk populations, success is relative. Dual-enrollment programs sometimes face a chilly reception from college faculty, who resist what they see as the encroachment of high schools onto their turf. (Unfortunately, concurrent-enrollment programs—in which the college courses are taught on the high school campus during the school day by high school teachers—tend not to have the same positive results for students [Jacobs, 2012]). They also tend to have relatively high administrative costs per student, as they employ "resource specialists" to shepherd the students personally through the program. Whether these programs will prove fiscally sustainable after the initial wave of grant money remains to be seen. To the extent that they start to bridge some of the cultural divide between the credit and noncredit sides of the house, though, they may do some real, if unintended, good for the colleges themselves.

Financial Aid

Financial aid is the lifeblood of most enrollment-driven colleges. My community college, like most, simply could not survive without it. (For the record, I was a financial aid student myself, and I strongly support increased financial aid for students at both the state and federal levels.) Financial aid helps the talented but broke, the smart kid whose parents don't make much, and the kid from the wrong side of the tracks have a shot at a better life. Ask college administrators across the country, and I suspect you'd get close to 100 percent agreement on that.

All of that said, though, financial aid brings several issues of its own.

Compliance with copious and ever shifting financial aid regulations is a serious drain of time and money. First, it's unspeakably complicated. The major federal programs alone—Pell grants, Guaranteed Student Loans, all the Title IV stuff—have exhaustive requirements for documentation and reporting. Students have to prove that they need the money, and one person's definition of "need" may not be another's. (This gets particularly tricky when you have divorced parents in the picture.) Setting a precise dollar figure on "need" can be particularly difficult when somebody's income varies wildly, whether due to seasonal or cyclical work, family or medical issues, or a tricky economy. By definition, it's also dependent on precise figures for tuition and fees, which are sometimes set relatively late in the spring, when state budgets are still in flux. And although demand for financial aid tends broadly to follow the economy, its availability tends to be countercyclical. It falls victim to budget cuts at precisely the moments it's most needed.

Second, the financial aid rules are constantly changing in response to shifts in the political winds. Student loan rules, for example, change with every presidential administration. After 9/11, rules for international students became far more complex. In the wake of some disturbing revelations about abuses in the for-profit sector, the federal government recently established a series of "gainful employment" rules that apply to certificate programs; those rules require much more tracking of students than had been required before. Now some states are starting to experiment, with federal encouragement, with shifting from financial aid based on attendance to financial aid based on "performance" (usually defined as graduation). The idea is to use aid to reduce student attrition rates. Whatever the merits of this shift, it's certain to impose still more tracking and reporting requirements on colleges that participate, and those come with costs.

Third, financial aid regulations lead to all manner of internal process changes within the academic side of the house, each of which brings the usual resistance and noncompliance. For example, in order to prevent financial aid from becoming a free federal subsidy for slacking, students who receive it are required to maintain enrollment and "satisfactory academic progress" (SAP) in their programs. SAP reporting encompasses both grades and attendance, which means that careful records need to be kept of both. That necessarily entails faculty cooperation.

The SAP requirement can also lead to perverse incentives. To maintain SAP, students are supposed to successfully complete two-thirds of the credits attempted in any given semester. Depending on how many credits a student is carrying, for example, she may be better off dropping a class in which she's struggling than she would be if she failed it. That leads to students who had a shot at a ninth-inning rally leaving the game early. Similarly, financial aid won't pay for a second attempt at a course in which the student earned a passing grade. This rule can wreak havoc in sequenced courses in which a student received a D, but a C or better is needed to continue in the sequence. I've been through debates on campus about whether to adjust the grading policy in a given sequence in light of financial aid rules; invariably, the faculty rebel, and the students lose.

When students stop showing up, faculty are supposed to keep good records of the last date of attendance (LDA). Amazingly, and for reasons I still don't understand, some of the most commonly used back-office IT systems still don't have an elegant way to record or report LDAs. And in the context of an online class, the last date of attendance isn't always obvious.

Financial aid is a form of what economists call "price discrimination," which entails charging different customers different amounts based on their apparent willingness or ability to pay. Price discrimination is the holy grail of private business, as pricing a good too high means sacrificing sales, and pricing it too low means leaving money on the table.[5] Higher education is able to engage in an unapologetic form of price discrimination and to claim the moral high ground while doing it. The bright side of that price discrimination is that it makes college available to students who otherwise couldn't afford it. If you believe in careers open to talent, this is no small thing.

Among people looking to cut support for financial aid, it has become popular to argue that the presence of a third-party payer tends to defeat price discipline. There may be some truth to this at low levels, but it's easy to overstate. For example, having over fifty million Americans uninsured hasn't led to price discipline in health care. (Perhaps more telling, the nearly complete absence of pet insurance hasn't led to price discipline in veterinary care, either [Warner, 2012].) If anything, limits on public financial aid have simply led to the flourishing of private lending.

Private Financial Aid

Over the last decade, college costs have risen faster than the availability of subsidized federal aid. Just as water finds any crack in a roof, private lenders rushed in to fill the cracks in financial aid. In 2010, we passed a remarkable milestone: accumulated student loan debt actually exceeded accumulated credit card debt. Unlike credit card debt, student loan debt can't be discharged in bankruptcy.

In the short term, from a college's perspective, the original source doesn't matter much. As long as we get paid, we're happy. But private lenders put students in a tough spot. In most federal student loans, students aren't charged interest while they're still in school. (Until 2012, the interest deferment continued for six months after graduation.) In most private loans, students are charged interest from the moment the loan originates. (The payments themselves are deferred, but when they come due, they include interest accrued during the student's enrollment.) Private loans also usually charge higher interest rates than federal loans, to cover the increased risk from their not being guaranteed.

Oddly, one thing that isn't an additional cost of private loans is profit. Federally subsidized loans are run through banks as middlemen, and the banks get a profit despite also getting origination fees and a guarantee of repayment. How that's anything but leeching is beyond me, but there it is.

Prior to 2012, I also saw a nontrivial number of students use aid-enabled enrollment as a way to get or keep health insurance. Many health insurers would allow parents to keep their adult children on the parents' coverage, as long as the adult children are enrolled in college full-time. I had students beg me to raise the caps on closed classes so they could get that coveted twelfth credit, which defined full-time status. I'm told that in the 1960s, young people used college enrollment to dodge the draft. Until 2012, they used it to get health insurance. In both cases, incentives that have nothing to do with the regular business of education are exerted distorting pressures on what we do. Students who used education to get financial aid, rather than the other way around, showed as attrition when they left, as if they were actually trying to complete a program and failed.

The financial aid system also has unintended effects on our ability to experiment. It was built on several assumptions—the academic calendar, the credit hour, clearly defined semesters—that may or may not make sense anymore, but that we aren't really free to change. I've run into these roadblocks repeatedly on my own campus even when attempting relatively basic changes, like the addition of a January intersession or a self-paced developmental math course.

In trying to put together a joint degree-completion program with a neighboring four-year college, I ran headfirst into the rule that a student can receive aid at only one school at a time. This means that a student taking courses at two colleges simultaneously, as in a joint program, becomes a monster headache for the financial aid office. It can be done, but only through a "consortial" agreement. If you want to watch a financial aid office director's eyes roll back into her head, drop the word "consortium" around her sometime.

Financial Aid as the New State Aid

At a fundamental level, financial aid is channeled through students rather than through colleges. This means that shifting resources from direct operating aid to financial aid actually increases the pressure on colleges to increase tuition. This isn't just opportunism, although that's certainly part of it. It's a basic mathematical fact.

This has consequences. The more heavily a public college relies on tuition and fees to sustain itself, the more closely its business model starts to resemble a traditional nonprofit private college. Small programs that cost significant dollars become harder to sustain, because the nontuition cushion becomes a progressively smaller portion of the budget. (At my own college, the part of the budget covered by the state appropriation went from half to one-third in just three years.) As the business model comes closer to that of a private college, so too will the tuition. It can't not.

Obviously, getting away from the clear political trends of the last few years would help. If states or counties would commit to reliably funding x percent of operating budgets each year, the tuition spiral would slow somewhat. But as long as the productivity issue goes unaddressed, the underlying problem will still be there.

Foundations

Although community colleges as a sector have attained nowhere near the level four-year colleges or universities have in their alumni-based fundraising, they've at least started trying.

The usual channel for alumni fundraising is a foundation. A foundation dedicated to the college, but with its own board of trustees, can allow donors to claim tax deductions for their gifts. It can also allow donors to "earmark" the uses of their gifts, which introduces issues of its own. Foundations keep budgets separate from the colleges to which they're dedicated, and can only make transfers for certain, very narrowly defined purposes.[6]

The most common use for foundation resources is student scholarships. Scholarships are great for students, because unlike student loans, they don't have to be repaid. But as with financial aid, money that goes into scholarships creates a gravitational pull toward higher tuition. *Money that comes in as operating aid can hold tuition down, but money that comes in as scholarships can only be fully captured by moving tuition up.*

That's especially true when you realize that many scholarships go unclaimed, sometimes for years at a time, because nobody eligible applied for them. Sometimes that's a marketing issue—would-be recipients just don't know about them—and sometimes it's timing, but it's often a function of the conditions donors put on scholarships. If you have to be a left-handed flute major from one of two towns, it may be years between eligible candidates.

Foundations usually try to steer donors to more inclusive sets of conditions, but ultimately, it's up to the donors. Every year, an embarrassing chunk of money goes unclaimed for exactly that reason. If the money went into the operating budget, that problem would be thoroughly solved.

GPA requirements can also be problematic at the community college level, as the best students are only there for two years. This means that by the time they've declared the right major and attained the right number of credits to qualify for scholarship help, they're out the door. Although it's lovely to help the student pay for the transfer school, it often means that money intended to find its way to the community college never actually does.

In some cases, foundation money *can* be used to offset some basic operational expenses. I've seen a Center for Teaching Excellence model, in which some portion of the travel funding for faculty was paid for by the foundation. I've also seen foundation money used for certain capital expenses, such as lab equipment. Because lab equipment and faculty travel would normally be funded out of the operating budget, these subventions actually help with the overall budget. But they remain exceptions. With most donations going to capital or to scholarships, they do nothing to reduce the rate of tuition increase. If anything, they may actually accelerate it a bit.

Reserves and Endowments

Many four-year colleges or universities have "endowment" models. An endowment is a portfolio of assets that generates income—from interest, dividends, appreciation, or some combination of these—that can be directed for specific uses on campus. Depending on the college, endowments can range from covering the bulk of the budget, as at Harvard, to little more than an aspiration. But the model is the same either way: principal is left untouched, and some portion of income is used to help sustain certain college operations.

Although you'd think that an endowment would double as a rainy-day fund, recent history suggests that this may not be true. To the extent that endowment funds are invested in, say, stocks, their value rises and falls with the market. In a reversal of the historical trend, the 2008–2010 recession actually hit elite institutions even harder than it hit everyone else, because the abrupt drop in equity values led to an abrupt drop in endowment income. When endowment income is half your budget, a severe one-year drop is painful. If your endowment is small enough that it doesn't matter much, then an abrupt drop in its value doesn't matter much, either.

Some community colleges have reserves, rather than endowments. If you think of endowments as long-term investments, think of reserves as the savings account you keep just to smooth out expensive months. Reserves are not intended primarily to generate income; they're really intended to fill in unexpected gaps in operating expenses.

The key difference between a reserve account and an endowment is that an endowment is typically intended to provide operating income through interest or investment earnings, whereas a reserve account is intended as a rainy-day fund.

Of course, one person's rainy day is another person's structural deficit. If a college's long-term path is economically unsustainable, there can be a temptation to paper over the gaps by spending out of reserves. This is a form of institutional suicide. Once reserves are spent, they're spent, so it's best not to use them to procrastinate about solving long-term problems. Spending from reserves makes sense for short sharp shocks, such as natural disasters or state cuts that land midyear. (Midyear cuts are worse than any other kind, as many of the expenses for the year have already been committed. Classes that start in January run into May, so once I've passed the January start of classes, in budgetary terms it might as well be May.)

Unfortunately, healthy reserves make ripe targets for state legislatures desperate for money. If a legislator is weighing the relative impact of cuts on different sectors, and one sector has millions in reserves while the other doesn't, it's easy to see why he'd choose the one with reserves. If you're sitting on millions, a legislator may believe, then you obviously don't need as much help.

From the college's perspective, this has the effect of punishing frugality. It's the macro version of "use it or lose it," and it effectively guarantees waste.

One way that colleges avoid losing it is by using it for nonoperating purposes, such as renovations or construction. Legislatures tend to like capital projects, because they are tangible and create construction jobs. Here again, it's easier to get money to build a building than it is to get money for people to work in it. If you can leverage your reserves with donations in return for naming rights, and maybe some state or federal matching grants, then the argument for construction is hard to refute. Build now, or take a deep cut in your appropriation in the next few years; you'd be stupid not to build. Let someone else worry about the parking.

Reserves create some tricky political issues on campus, too. Faculty unions like to think of reserves as money that should be spent on them, and they like to quote reserve figures to cast doubt on rationales for austerity. But money spent on raises or new positions is recurring and even compounding, which means that unless you can count on the reserves going on forever, it's a poor strategy. At least with construction, once the building is done, it's done.

The Bottom Line

The upshot of all of these limitations is that community college operating budgets are not merely tight but likely to get tighter for the foreseeable future. And the tightness has nothing to do with evil administrators hoarding the gold, or NCAA athletics, or climbing walls, or any of the usual suspects in popular discussion. The tightness is structural, and it's reinforced through several disconnected choices that all point in the same direction. In the absence of a major change to the underlying drivers, I'd expect to see current trends continue—cost-shifting to students, higher-than-inflation tuition increases, increased reliance on adjuncts. If we want to interrupt or even reverse these trends, we'll have to make fundamental, structural changes, such as those I suggest in Chapter Six.

COMMUNITY COLLEGE ADMINISTRATION

WHO DOES WHAT

DEANS DON'T GET MUCH RESPECT IN THE MEDIA. Dean Wormer, from *Animal House*, had one great line ("Fat, drunk, and stupid is no way to go through life, son . . ."), but wound up cuckolded and flailing in a parade float. Larry Miller's dean in *The Nutty Professor* got sodomized by a giant hamster. Dean Pelton on the TV series *Community* is an incompetent micromanager with a fondness for cross-dressing who is taken seriously by absolutely no one.

On the blogs, it's even worse. As a side effect of the awful job market for aspiring faculty, caricatures of deans abound. They're usually presented as a cross between Snidely Whiplash and Scrooge McDuck, cackling over the ill-gotten fruits of underpaying adjuncts. The idea is that deans are evil, overpaid figureheads who spend their time centralizing power in their own hands, living off the labor of others, and hopping frantically from campus to campus in the single-minded pursuit of their own career advancement.

The day-to-day reality of midlevel administration is far more pedestrian—and important—than that. To actually understand the job, it's important first to understand the structure of the organization and the dean's place in it.

The Community College Hierarchy

Although the "dean" title is often used throughout the organization for pay-grade reasons, the classic academic dean usually sits at a specific point in the hierarchy. A typical organization chart will look something like this:

Board of trustees

President

Vice presidents—academic affairs, student affairs, administration and finance, corporate and community programs (continuing ed), foundation

Deans—academic divisions, admissions, financial aid, HR

Department chairs

Full-time faculty

Adjunct or part-time faculty

Each of these roles is distinctive, although in practice they sometimes shade into each other.

Board of Trustees

The board of trustees is the ultimate authority unique to the college. (The college also answers to the state government, the federal government, a

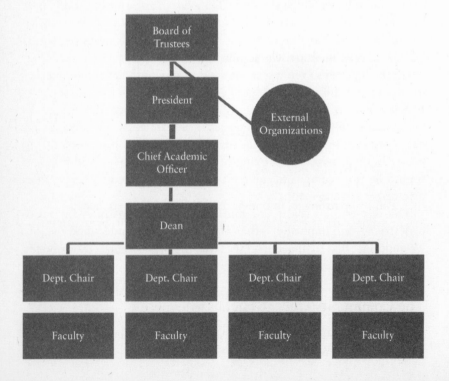

regional accrediting agency, and the like, but none of those is unique to one college. The board is usually unique to one college, though some states, like Tennessee and Virginia, have statewide boards.)

The board is charged with selecting, evaluating, and, when necessary, replacing the president. It also maintains high-level oversight of the college budget and has final approving authority on tuition or fee changes. (In some states, the state sets tuition and the campus sets fees. Where that happens, tuitions tend to lag, and fees outstrip them.) It formally approves lower-level personnel hires, though that's usually a rubber-stamp function. It also sets certain college policies, like its treatment of undocumented students or same-sex partners of employees. Finally, it usually takes an active role in fundraising and "friendraising" for the college.

Ideally, the board will be diverse by race and gender, but uniform in comprising intelligent, successful people who are committed to higher education. And sometimes that's the case. Boards can go haywire, though. Common sources of board dysfunction include the following:

- **Micromanaging.** A good board delegates to the college administration and doesn't second-guess operational decisions on a routine basis. If it does, staff will quickly figure out that it can do end runs around management; before long, nobody will know what the rules are.

- **Incoherence.** A publicly divided board creates openings for all manner of mischief. Worse, a board that changes its mind based on who showed up at that month's meeting makes lower-level constancy impossible.

- **Political agendas.** Some board members forget the point of the office and use the bully pulpit to grandstand in service of their personal political ambitions. These people tend to make a big splash early and to move on before the waves caused by those splashes have reached their full destructive potential.

- **Political patronage.** In one-party jurisdictions where board members are selected by local or state government, board seats are sometimes handed out as consolation prizes for loyal party activists. In one-party jurisdictions, this can leave tenacious but unhelpful board members in place for decades. The need to appease the occasional true believer can lead to decisions being made for the wrong reasons.

- **Cults of personality.** Some boards buy too deeply into the myth of the Perfect Leader and assume that all problems can be solved by

finding the perfect college president. By mistaking structural problems for personnel problems, they leave the structural problems
untreated. Typically these boards overpay and overpromise and
then either act quickly out of disappointment that the Chosen One
couldn't defy gravity, or get snookered by a charismatic narcissist
until the wheels fall off. Either way, the college suffers.

The better boards manage to avoid most of these pitfalls most of the
time. Instead, they understand their role as supporters of the college, eval-
uators of the president, and makers of very high level policy decisions.
They leave management to administration.

The President

The community college president's job is changing rapidly, and so is the
cast of characters. This is a fairly new development. Since the national
explosion of community college building that started around 1960 and
ended in the mid-1970s, the generation that poured in during the boom
years is only now starting to age out of the system. But it's not going
quietly; at this point, the second-most-common previous job for a community college president is . . . community college president! (I've actually
seen candidates for presidencies disparaged as "lacking presidential experience.") Once someone is in the club, it's not at all unusual for him
(women hold about one-third of community college presidencies, though
their share is climbing) to hold a succession of presidencies over a decade
or more (Cook and Kim, 2012).

Community college presidents have historically had very different
responsibilities from their counterparts in other sectors of higher education. Unlike their counterparts at private colleges, they haven't had to
focus much on philanthropy or private fundraising. (That's changing, but
the difference is still substantial.) Unlike their counterparts at public universities, they haven't had to woo state legislatures or governors. Their
primary foci in the past could have been working with the board and
with various community agencies and leaders. If they chose, they could
also get involved with issues internal to the college.

Now, the picture is different.

In states with local or county systems, presidents could once devote
relatively little attention to state government. This is no longer true, even
though state aid typically makes up a smaller percentage of the college
budget than it once did.

With state budgets increasingly constrained, community colleges cannot assume—if they ever could—that next year's appropriation will be

this year's plus a little. And with legislators sold on the usefulness of community colleges for workforce development, even as they're unsold on the idea of actually paying for it, presidents now have to be much more intentional and thoughtful about cultivating the right impression. That's especially true as numerous third parties start filling the information void with statistics of their own, reflecting their own purposes.

Although presidents have to be careful in choosing their causes with legislators, they have considerable freedom to frame issues. In many ways, this is one of their most important roles. Would increased community college funding represent a black hole or an investment in the state's future? A president who can make the case for her college effectively—both with politicians and with the public at large—is a real asset.

On the philanthropic side, community colleges no longer simply cede the territory to the four-year schools. Of necessity, many community colleges have established foundations to cultivate donors. This means that presidents have to develop a new skill set.

Although they haven't reached the same level as the four-year colleges, in which the running joke is that the president reports to the development office, community college presidents do have to pay more attention to private donors than they did in the past. If current fiscal trends broadly continue, I expect to see this aspect of the role increase over time.

Presidents are the public face of a college, with all that implies. A president should expect to be a public ambassador of the college at all manner of functions, and should conduct herself accordingly. A president who shoots from the lip, has a weakness for overspending or abusing the perquisites of power, or simply can't bring herself to be a reliably professional public presence will fail in the role.

Presidents also have the last word on difficult internal issues, such as layoffs or terminations. Successful presidents manage to know the very worst about the people who work at the college, yet still sincerely believe in the value of the college and the importance of its mission. And they know which part to discuss in public.

Internally, presidents have a different kind of bully pulpit. Savvy presidents use that pulpit to call attention to a very short list of priorities—three or fewer is ideal—and to stick to that same short list for years. Predictability can be a virtue. To the extent that presidents take steps to ensure that the publicly announced priorities are actually given preference internally at budget time, the consistency will gradually convey the message that the college actually follows through on what it says.

Presidents can misplay this role in several ways.

One way is to ignore it. I once worked for a president who never used the bully pulpit for anything substantive. Every speech was either a synopsis of current events or the standard "education is important." He seemed to delegate internal priority setting to his vice presidents.

The problem there, of course, is that the cabinet officers don't have the same bully pulpit. In the absence of a clear direction, the various vice presidents simply went their own ways.

A second way is to be inconsistent. I worked for another president whose attention was captured by a different shiny object each week. When the folks below learn that there's a flavor-of-the-month system, they learn to simply ride out whatever they don't like. They calculated, correctly, that if you don't like the current flavor, you can just wait for the next one. It bred cynicism, passivity, and fatalism.

Finally, of course, there's the substitution of ego for mission. When presidential leadership becomes more about the president than about leadership, the college will struggle. This is dishearteningly common, and probably a hazard of any position of authority.

Vice Presidents

The president's other main internal responsibility is to hire vice presidents, who have day-to-day responsibility for internal operations. Vice presidents typically turn over at considerably higher rates than presidents; one recent study claimed that the average length in office for an academic vice president is only three years (Cook and Kim, 2012). (The study noted that common reasons for leaving were retirement, burnout, accepting a higher position elsewhere, and falling victim to a purge of the old regime when a new president arrives.)

Some colleges have an in-between position called a provost. Typically a provost is the first-among-equals among the vice presidents, although in some larger contexts, the various vice presidents will report to the provost. In most provost systems, the provost is essentially the chief operating officer of the college, leaving the president free to tend almost exclusively to external relations. My own experience, though, has been at colleges without provosts.

Depending on local culture, the vice president is typically somewhere between a mini-president and an office manager. I've found that the most effective ones concern themselves primarily with harmonizing the overall direction of the college as set by the president with the operational constraints set by limited resources and collective bargaining agreements. That will usually mean considerable attention paid to processes, incentives, and precedents. A successful vice president will set a climate in which constructive change is rewarded and inward-looking politicking is not.

From my own experience and observation, the single most crucial note I'd give any vice president or dean is this: actions don't explain themselves. I've seen perfectly reasonable and wise decisions land with a thud because the faculty or staff did not understand the reasons behind them. College faculty and staff are smart and creative people; when an explanation isn't offered, they're more than capable of generating their own. The problem is that their own explanations are frequently far more sinister than the truth.

For example, at one college at which I worked, the course scheduler decided one semester that it made sense to locate the math classes in the new building on the edge of campus. The rooms in this building had larger chalkboards; the idea was to give the math faculty more space on which to do equations. He didn't communicate his rationale, though, and when the schedule came out, the math department—which was largely Jewish—accused him of anti-Semitism for making them walk farther to class. A scheduling idea that could have been accepted or rebutted on its merits instead became an ugly exchange of charges and countercharges that never had to happen.

As I mentioned, vice presidents often lack the same access to the bully pulpit that presidents have. Open meetings are a fine way to compensate for that—if they don't fall victim to scheduling conflicts and interpersonal drama. This is where technology can help.

As I will discuss further in the next chapter, an on-campus blog can make a world of difference. When an issue comes along, a blog gives an administrator a chance to put the reasoning process out there for all to see. It can be a useful way to solicit constructive input, as it doesn't fall prey to scheduling conflicts, and the written form allows for careful phrasing. It's useful in the idea formation phase, as it offers the opportunity to frame a discussion—what the key considerations are, what the relevant constraints are—and to gain access to perspectives from across campus. It can also be useful in the "announcement" phase, as it allows you to package the decision with an explanation of the reasons for it.

Department Chairs

Let's skip the dean's slot for the moment and look at the job of department chair. In some settings, the department chairs are considered supervisory, making decisions about performance evaluation and even the distribution of merit raises. In other settings, the department chair deals mostly with logistics, and leaves the supervisory role to the dean. Depending on local context, the department chairs may be elected by the faculty, appointed by the dean, or on an internal rotation.

Each selection method brings its issues. Deanly selection offers at least the possibility of a relatively consistent message throughout the college, but it only works if the selection process is real (and if enough options are available). Election helps the chair get around charges of being a puppet of the administration, but it can easily result in chairs who don't know or care about the details of administration. Rotation takes the flaws of election and doubles down on them; if a chair is neither selected for ability nor penalized for poor performance, the only way to make the system work consistently is to make the chairs mostly irrelevant.

At my first community college, the department chairs had tremendous supervisory authority and were appointed to annual contracts by the division dean. In practice, the chairs held their positions for life; when I got there, two of the chairs in my division were in their third decade of chairing. Because surviving twenty-five consecutive annual appointments creates a certain expectation, the chairs were effectively (though not technically) tenured in their roles. Predictably, this led to severe siloing, as each chair guarded her turf jealously. It also rendered the deans largely irrelevant for many purposes, as the authority that most faculty actually feared was the chair.

I'm no fan of that structure. Among other things, it led to some of the more entrenched chairs operating their departments as political machines. On the rare occasions when full-time faculty positions came along, several of the chairs made it known quite clearly that they had established an informal take-a-number system among the adjuncts, based on a combination of seniority, fealty, and personal taste. When a position came along, chairs would refer to it as "so-and-so's job" and treat the search as a distasteful formality to be discharged as quickly and painlessly as possible.

From the chair's perspective, the ability to distribute these coveted goodies was the source of considerable authority. Adjuncts could be strung along for years in the vague hope of currying favor and getting to be next in line. When the occasional favored one managed to break into the inner circle, the message sent to the other adjuncts was clear: please the chair and you'll be rewarded. Alternately, when the dean intervened to the detriment of the chair's favored one, the chair's authority was called into question. At that point, the accusations of "administrative meddling" flew.

Of course, "fixed" searches raise severe legal and ethical issues. Searches are expensive, in terms of both direct costs (advertising, transportation of candidates) and indirect costs (time and energy). To spend resources on a search for which the fix is in is both wasteful and unethical.

There's also a very real issue of inbreeding. By definition, the local adjunct pool is local. It will reflect the demographics of the people who live in the immediate area and who can afford to work for peanuts. (At my first community college, we got a lot of executive's wives.) To the extent that seniority plays into it, you're favoring people whose graduate training may be decades behind them and who have not been able to keep up with developments in the field. You'll draw disproportionately from the local graduate programs, which means that existing pedagogical blind spots will be reproduced. You'll give false hope to external candidates who devote time and energy to going through a futile exercise. And racial or ethnic diversity will be even harder to achieve than it otherwise is, unless you live in one of a few specific regions.

In strong-chair settings, it's easy for chairs to become petty tyrants. When that happens, the job of the dean is to bring the collegewide perspective to matters that chairs would often prefer to keep local. That means attending to the union contract, if any; affirmative action guidelines; collegewide priorities, policies, and protocols; competing needs from other departments or programs; and how things will look to the public when they get out.

Effective department chairs have two major roles: translator and project manager. The translator role involves helping faculty understand what the administration is trying to do, and helping the administration understand the valid concerns that faculty raise. This means avoiding the temptation, in most cases, to choose sides. Some chairs have a hard time with that, understanding their roles instead as advocates for their departments. Paradoxically, the chairs who become the most effective advocates are the ones who don't set out to be advocates. They earn credibility with the administration by doing the core job well; folks with credibility have a much easier time making (or preventing) change.

The project manager role is more commonly where chairs fail. Although it's tempting to imagine department chairs as wielding great power, in truth, much of what they do involves the nitty-gritty details of interviewing and scheduling adjuncts, making sure textbook orders are submitted on time, and keeping the photocopier running. I've seen wonderful professors become awful department chairs because they can't make themselves care about the administrivia of the role. That's understandable, certainly, but the details matter when they're ignored.

The Dean's Job: Make Juggling Look Easy

The essence of being a dean is knowing how to balance. The trustees set broad policy, usually in conjunction with some sort of state system. The president has the option of setting a few top priorities internally (though I've seen presidents both overshoot and undershoot the mark). Vice presidents try to operationalize those top priorities. Meanwhile, faculty and individual departments usually try to ignore the broad goals and pursue their own agendas. (Faculty largely think of themselves as independent operators, on loan to the college from their scholarly discipline.) Deans have the lucky task of mediating among all of those.

Part of the stress of middle management is the toxic combination of responsibility without authority. That's particularly true when dealing with tenured faculty, and even more so when dealing with tenured faculty in a unionized setting during a budget crunch. In other words, most of the time.

A successful dean connects the collegewide issues with the concerns of individual departments and faculty, and helps them work together in support of the college's mission. Explaining and listening are major parts of the process. The process can be difficult when the power to actually change something rests at a higher level, but the effort is worth it.

Bean Counter: Managing Budgets

Academic departments usually have their own budgets, managed by the chair. The dean's job involves making sure that the budgets are done correctly and that processes and limits are honored. These tasks are usually fairly easy in areas like the social sciences, where the classes don't usually require specialized equipment or labs, and more difficult in physical sciences and studio art, where the facilities and budgets are more complicated.

Deans usually have budgets of their own, which are much more limited than many faculty tend to believe. These often have "contingency" lines, which is money set aside for unforeseen emergencies. (The more conspiratorially minded sometimes call them "slush funds," at least until they need the money themselves.)

Contingency lines are remarkably hard to manage well. By definition, they're hard to allocate. If the fiscal year runs the standard July to June, how confident can you be in, say, October, that nothing bad will happen for the next eight months?

Midyear budget cuts are uniquely challenging. As mentioned in Chapter Two, colleges are required, more often than can reasonably be excused, to absorb budget cuts from the state or county in the middle of the budget year. Because most of the college budget is labor, and because for fiscal purposes a semester started is a semester finished, unused contingency funds make very tempting targets for midyear rescissions. If you define "budget cut" as a contingency, then that makes perfect sense.

But it creates a local incentive to spend it while you have it. Too much austerity, paradoxically enough, actually breeds inefficiency.

Outside of contingency lines, deans quickly find that most of their budget is already spoken for and effectively out of their control.

Manager of Faculty Workloads

In a teaching institution, as opposed to a research institution, the bulk of the full-time faculty workload will be teaching and academic advising, with some level of "service" (which is usually defined as committee work). If you're lucky, the union contract or faculty handbook will be relatively specific about faculty workloads. I've seen them expressed in credit hours, and I've also seen multivariate equations that take into account credit hours, "preps," class sizes, and so on.

When you need institutional work done that goes beyond the standard expectation for committee service, the usual mechanism is "released time" or "reassigned time." In essence, it's a reduction in teaching load in exchange for an increase in service load. The idea is that someone who usually teaches five classes would have more time for service if one or two of those classes were taken away. Common uses for released time include work on accreditation documents, chairing a department, coordination of larger or specialized academic programs, oversight of a lab or studio, or ad hoc projects.

When there's room in the budget, the dean (or chief academic officer) usually has some discretion over the allocation of released time. A smart dean makes the expectations of the duties being bought explicit, and builds in some sort of assessment mechanism. Otherwise, after a few years, the released time becomes a de facto entitlement.

Typically, the direct cost to the institution of released time is the cost of the adjunct who teaches the course instead, so released time is a way to pay adjunct wages for administrative work.[1] The college likes it because it gets proven people on the cheap. The full-time faculty like it because it reduces their teaching load and breaks the monotony of teaching the same intro course over and over again. The adjuncts like it because it provides jobs. The outside world doesn't really understand it, so you're occasionally subject to demagoguery about it ("You have people earning full pay teaching part-time!"), but it's actually a valuable tool. The alternative—hiring more full-time administrators—is usually both prohibitively expensive and politically toxic.

Course Scheduler

Released time is not the only tool in the kit. Depending on how much you want to micromanage, it's possible to use course scheduling as an incentive or punishment—though I don't advocate this strategy. Most schedules have some slots that nobody really wants to cover ("Friday, 8 AM. Who's game?") but that have to be done. Different faculty have different scheduling preferences, often based on family issues or commuting patterns. If you really want to mess with someone, you can assign a schedule that would make his life hell. But when you do that, you risk earning a reputation for being petty and vindictive. And students will usually get less than the best experience, because the instructor is there grudgingly. If a given section gets to be known as administrative Siberia, then whoever gets it in a given semester will assume, often incorrectly, that she's in the doghouse. You'll wind up generating needless conflict. It's better to wall off scheduling from punishment.

Scheduling raises other issues as well. In theory, you schedule the full-time faculty first and then fill in the gaps with adjuncts. In reality, though, it's more of a balancing act. Many departments have wonderful long-term adjuncts they want to keep around and keep happy, even if they can't give them full-time positions. These folks usually have some pretty specific time constraints, often involving working concurrently at other colleges or in other positions. (Hence the name "freeway flyers.") There's a valid argument to the effect that you should schedule these folks first, then fill in the full-timers around them. The full-timers are paid to be available whenever; the adjuncts are around only when they're around.

In many settings, the informal division of labor will have department chairs scheduling the adjuncts, and deans scheduling full-time faculty. That can make sense when the number of sections grows large, but it places a real premium on trust and communication between the dean and the chair.

A savvy dean will also look at preps, or course preparations. If a professor has three sections of Math 120 and two sections of Math 150, she has two preps. If she has one section each of Math 120, 125, 135, 140, and 150, she has five preps. All else being equal, five sections with two preps is less work than five sections with five preps. To the extent that you can control the number, it's usually best to keep the preps to two (or three at most) per professor per semester. (Some collective bargaining agreements set maxima for preps.) If one of the preps is entirely new to the professor, it's best to keep everything else as straightforward as possible that semester.

You also have to consider historical patterns around which courses always fill and which are crapshoots. If an adjunct's class doesn't "make," you just don't run the class. But if a full-timer's class doesn't make, you have to adjust the schedule to keep that person at a full load. In times of volatile enrollment, this can be a real issue.

The decision to cancel sections with low enrollment is thankless, and impossible to get right. Typically, a few weeks before the semester starts, the deans have to decide—based on the enrollment numbers available at the time, as well as hunches and historical patterns—which sections are unlikely to make the local minimum enrollment to run. (At my college, for most courses, the minimum is fifteen. Exceptions include the last course in a sequence and courses with specialized labs or studios.) If you don't prorate faculty compensation for courses with low enrollment—we don't— then you need to set certain minima to remain economically viable. When classroom space is limited, there's also the issue of fairness to other students. If a section with five students is displacing what could have been a section of thirty, the harm accrues both to the college (in lost revenue) and to twenty-five students who couldn't get the class they wanted.

The dilemma with course cancellations is that they necessarily involve peering into the near future and making educated guesses. I've had faculty whose classes were cancelled complain bitterly that they would have filled if only they'd stayed open long enough. That's impossible to prove one way or the other, so people who decide to be offended can stay offended for a long time.

Online courses offer a partial solution for niche classes—the kind with maybe ten or twenty students across the entire college who want it in a given semester. It's unlikely that all those students will be free on the same day and time, but if you can catch them all in a single online section, then you've made the niche course economically viable. (In my observation, colleges haven't generally used online courses this way, even though it would make sense if they did.)

Diplomat: Handling Faculty Evaluations

Evaluating full-time faculty is a core function for most academic deans, and it's one of the hardest parts of the job. For all the drama involved in doing it, I've been consistently surprised at how little it has usually mattered.

In the community colleges I've seen, raises have been contractual and across the board. Promotion steps have been small, when they've existed at all. And faculty with tenure and union protection are effectively untouchable as long as they don't commit felonies or sleep with students. Some will still take grave offense at any meaningful criticism, though, even if the substantive impact of that criticism is nil.

If you have a collective bargaining agreement, it's pretty much a given that the format and criteria for evaluation will be spelled out in some detail. However, be on the lookout for the graveyard of deans everywhere: *past practice*.

Past practice is the status given to unofficial and unwritten, but generally observed, ways of doing things. It's similar to "precedent" in a legal setting; you can overturn it, but the burden of proof is on you. By definition, it isn't written down anywhere, so if you aren't careful, you'll only discover it when someone claims that you're in violation. Building trust up front and asking a lot of questions are the best defense. Otherwise, the traps have been set, and you'll walk right into them.

One of those traps is a legacy of grade inflation for employee evaluations. Department chairs have told me to my face that they've rated their own secretaries unrealistically high for years. They do it because there aren't any merit raises anyway, and in a setting in which you can neither reward nor fire people, there doesn't seem to be much payoff for criticism. They use effusive praise to keep the peace.

The problem with that, of course, is that it renders the evaluations useless as professional development tools. Worse, it can feed an arrogance and sense of entitlement such that, after a while, you just can't tell employees anything. When you've been told for a decade or more that you're utterly wonderful but underpaid, it can be difficult to hear that you need to change. In that setting, it's much easier just to shoot the messenger; typically that will take the form of grievances.

When evaluating employees who have performance issues, the dean is caught between two imperatives. The local cultural imperative typically favors leniency, if not outright grade inflation. (I've actually had an employee in tears when she received "exceeds expectations" rather than "far exceeds expectations" in a single category.) But the legal imperative goes exactly the other way. If you get to the point where you must sanction an employee for performance, you need an extensive paper trail. (Lawyers say "document, document, document" with the same fervor with which realtors say "location, location, location.") And an evaluation that seems bracingly candid by local cultural standards ("You only got a 'meets expectations'?!?!") will seem like weak tea in court. ("If she meets expectations, then what's the problem?") When the sanctioned employee makes the inevitable retaliatory claims of discrimination, the goodwill shown on previous evaluations will be used against you.

I've had several cases in which I inherited a long-standing, low-performing employee, but the paper trail was laudatory because my predecessor(s) didn't want the headache. Until the courts start to compensate for the reality of grading on a local curve, deans and other administrators would be well advised to tread carefully.

With all these considerations in place, evaluations have to be done strategically rather than candidly. Keep in mind the legal weight that evaluations carry, and the very real objection of pointlessness in upsetting someone who can't be terminated. That's not to say that you should simply roll over and perpetuate the culture of everybody being practically perfect in every way, but it does suggest a strategy of very deliberately choosing your battles.

Bearer of Bad News: Assessment

"Assessment" is a dirty word in faculty circles, but it matters. Over the past decade or so, it has become a binding expectation from the various regional accreditors. At the simplest level, it's an attempt to determine whether a given program or activity is achieving its goals. (At a more cynical level, it's an attempt for the higher education industry to show that it can regulate itself, so that it doesn't need external regulation.)

Outcomes assessment is intended to function as a reality check. Are graduates of a given program actually capable of doing what the college assumes they're capable of doing? If not, if something is missing or weak, what is the college going to do to address it? And how will it know if the new strategy is working?

At the conceptual level, outcomes assessment is hard to object to. In practice, though, many faculty find outcomes assessment intrusive, burdensome, and vaguely insulting; I've frequently heard it described as a stalking horse for an agenda of standardization. Negotiating the gap between a concept that makes good sense and deep-seated faculty objections is the enviable job of the dean.

At several campuses now, I've seen faculties go through the five Kübler-Ross stages (1969 [1997]) in dealing with outcomes assessment.

The first stage is denial. "We already do assessment! We give grades!" Like most knee-jerk objections, this misses the point. Grades measure student performance in individual courses. Outcomes assessment is supposed to capture institutional performance at the curricular level. Say that the English Department does a great job of teaching the literature classes it loves to teach, but simply refuses to teach poetry. Student grades may be high in the classes actually offered, but the curriculum will have a hole in it. Outcomes assessment properly done will capture the difference and will give an opening for a serious discussion of whether and how to address the gaps that have been identified.

Next comes anger. "This is just make-work! If you want better outcomes, give us better students, more money, and smaller classes!" The fallacy in these arguments is that they assume a 1:1 correlation between inputs and outputs. Worse, in the context of a chronically underfunded, open-door institution, they suggest fatalism. They use the perfect as the enemy of the good. Unless you're willing to argue with a straight face that this is actually the best of all possible worlds, this objection is simply selfish.

As the discussion continues, faculty shift to bargaining. "We'll need released time to do this right." Unlike the first two stages, this one at least opens the door for action. There's also some truth to some claims. If you want a department to devote extra time to extra evaluations of student papers, say, you'll need to address the impact on workload one way or another. The savvy dean will welcome this stage and make a point of rewarding the early adopters. But watch out for the classic move of setting impossible conditions: "To do this right, we'll need a full staff of full-time people, no transfer students, and a nationally normed test that isn't standardized." This is just a high-minded way of saying no. It's a variation on "Let's refer this intractable problem to a committee" as a way of making the problem go away. It's dishonesty masked as high standards. Don't fall for it.

Depression comes next. In academia, this is usually manifest in the repeated invocation of the magic phrase "Faculty morale is low." (Full disclosure: I've spent my entire adult life in and around higher education, at several different institutions and in several different roles. I have never, not once, heard someone say "Faculty morale is high." Many grains of salt are advised.) As with the bargaining stage, you should hear people out and address the more reasonable suggestions, but don't lose sight of the ultimate goal.

Finally comes acceptance. At this point, people start to realize that there really is a point to the enterprise, and they start analyzing the data and using them as the basis for decisions. If they're really clever, they even build assessment mechanisms into the next generation of revisions, to shorten the cycle of data collection and analysis. This is where you may see actual improvements.

The smart dean will make a point of highlighting successes at this stage, and calling attention (and resources) to the first programs that do this well. The smart dean will also avoid the common mistake of punishing candor. If valid assessment results show that real gaps exist—which they almost certainly will—then addressing them offers a chance for real progress. Demanding that early rounds of assessment result in nothing but upbeat findings will defeat the purpose, and guarantee more (and more justified) resistance in the future.

Finally, of course, the point is to "close the loop" by using the results of assessment to actually make changes to improve student outcomes. That could mean anything from changing the cluster of courses in the major to tweaking prerequisites to adding common assignments. Whatever is chosen—and I can't emphasize strongly enough that the choice itself should be left to the faculty—the point is to use assessment to identify gaps, try various things to fill those gaps, and then assess how well the new interventions work. The ultimate goal is to improve student success.

Done well, outcomes assessment holds the promise of helping colleges do what they do better. But the hurdles are several.

First, by its very nature, outcomes assessment implies distrust of traditional practice. Until recently, in many programs, the faculty have had the last word as to whether what they're doing is working or not. This has led to a well-worn culture of deference to credentials combined with a bad habit of blaming students. Outcomes assessment is based on the possibility that the emperor has no clothes. Of course, some actually don't, and their resistance is to be expected.

Second, there's a basic workload issue. If outcomes assessment is labor intensive and doesn't come with significant new resources, it's just one more thing to do. Given how hard many faculty already work with community college teaching loads, there's some real validity to this complaint.

Third is fear of a No Child Left Behind–style move to standardized tests. Given the tone deafness of many in the legislative branch, this fear is not to be dismissed out of hand. For the record, I agree that for higher ed to go this route would be catastrophic for all involved, as standardization defeats both specialization and content innovation. But given that the need for accountability is real, there's a solid argument for self-directed assessment mechanisms as an alternative to something standardized and legislatively imposed.

Fourth is fear that poor student performance will be held against individual faculty. Again, depending on how the assessment is implemented and what the local administration's agenda actually is, this fear can't necessarily be dismissed out of hand. But the remedy for it is not to hold your breath until assessment goes away. It's to get faculty involved in designing it, helping shape it in ways that ensure that the more sinister applications can't come to pass.

Besides, there's actually a strong institutional argument for not using assessment to single out low-performing faculty. If I know that Professor Smith consistently gets better results than Professor Jones, what, exactly, can I do with that? I can't scale it by cloning Professor Smith. But if I know that, say, students in college algebra do well with factoring but poorly with fractions, then I can suggest that the folks who design the developmental math curricula focus more on fractions. That information can lead to something the college can scale.

Paradoxically, a context-specific design will actually help with scalability. In other words, standardized assessment designs are less likely to lead to large-scale change than more locally sensitive designs are. That's because large-scale change depends crucially on faculty acceptance of the findings. If the faculty believe, rightly or wrongly, that the findings were artifacts of asking the wrong questions, they'll reject them. The way around this is to engage faculty up front in designing the assessment mechanism. That means spending some money up front to give course releases, and not getting too prescriptive about what the faculty devise. If the mechanism is developed by local faculty and in harmony with local culture, then the results will be much more likely to be taken seriously. You won't be able to close the loop if the faculty reject the instrument.

Program Evaluator

Programmatic assessment is usually somewhat easier. For example, the advising center argues for more staff and money to move to an intrusive advisement model. You allocate some resources, spelling out in advance the criteria and data you'll use in a year or two to measure whether it succeeded. If it did succeed, great; maybe you even expand it. If it didn't, you reallocate those resources to other projects that might succeed.

In some areas, this is so easy that there isn't much to say about it. If your admissions numbers are down while everyone else's around you are up, it's fair to ask the admissions director some hard questions.

As with outcomes assessment, though, part of the problem is appending assessment measures after the fact to something that was designed initially without assessment in mind. (If I had a nickel for every time I've heard a variation on "We can't capture that information, since the data weren't coded that way," I'd be a wealthy man.) There's also an inevitable time lag between the intervention and the availability of the results, as well as the obvious fact that pure control groups don't exist in nature. Was this year's enrollment increase the result of the new admissions protocols, the new academic programs, the more efficient financial aid office, the new marketing campaign, the failures of the college two towns over, or the recession? Good luck teasing out those variables on the fly.

(The ability to get relatively comfortable with working with incomplete and flawed data required a significant attitude shift when I went from faculty to administration. In grad school, I was trained to poke holes in weak data, to look for unwarranted logical leaps and false assumptions, and to avoid jumping to conclusions based on partial information. In administration, I have to put my misgivings aside and do all of those things. The owl of Minerva spreads its wings at dusk, but we usually can't wait that long. Decisions have to be made quickly and in a context of limited and flawed information. That's especially true when considering that the decisions that really count are about the future.)

To the extent that you can at least specify your metrics in advance, though, you can reduce the likelihood of decisions happening entirely randomly, and you can speed up the process at the same time.

Ambassador at Large

Although presidents are the formal public face of the college, deans and vice presidents frequently represent the college in making deals with other institutions. This involves a delicate blend of diplomacy, fiscal realism, and marketing.

In most cases, the initial approach is relatively easy. In dealing with four-year institutions, for example, the sheer fact of representing a feeder school puts you in a good position. In those conversations, the trick is simply not to overpromise. Pace what you say, and don't be afraid to use variations on "Let me get back to you." It's better to move slowly and get it right than to earn a reputation for being unreliable.

The bane of the ambassador is the spontaneous public speech. Most administrators at the level of dean and above run a variation on what I call the Rubber Chicken Circuit, in which they make appearances at various functions as a representative of the college. More than once I've found myself asked to "say a few words" on the spot, with no idea that I would be expected to speak.

The savvy dean will have a few "set pieces" at the ready, usually involving anecdotes. It's a good idea, too, to get a sense of the unique identity of the organization hosting the function. Flattering the audience is usually a good move. And when all else fails—which sometimes happens—fall back on the adage beloved of speech teachers everywhere: if you can't be great, be brief.

Academic Leader

I've heard deans and chief academic officers described as academic leaders, but in practice, few faculty like to be led. The term "academic leader" is usually used as a criticism when the speaker wants to attack the dean, but lacks anything more specific.

That said, there are moments when deans and vice presidents can exercise something like academic leadership.

For example, deans should not be shy about publicly and conspicuously supporting the faculty in its attempt to maintain academic standards. This will become more important as more external constituencies weigh in on graduation rates, retention rates, and the like. Many faculty perceive those pressures, rightly or wrongly, as veiled threats to lower their grading standards. Taking pains to reassure the faculty that their academic judgment will be supported—and then actually following through on it—is real academic leadership.

Less conspicuously, deans are barraged with student requests for grade changes, requirement waivers, and the like. As tempting as it can be to appease a loud and angry student to make him go away, a savvy dean will understand how deeply demoralizing it is to a professor to reward a student who goes over her head. That's not to say that one should never side with a student in a dispute, but it is to suggest that the burden of proof falls squarely on the student. The dean cannot grade every paper and is not a subject-matter expert in everything. Students talk to each other; if you reward end runs around faculty, you will get end runs around faculty. Academic integrity will suffer, the faculty will rightly hate you, and you will never get out from under. It's best to keep in mind the consequences of precedent. I have routinely upheld faculty decisions on academic matters, even when I've personally had misgivings about them or felt strongly that in the same situation, I would have handled it differently. Appeals are not do-overs; the burden of proof rises far above the level of mere disagreement.

In an appeal, a dean should keep in mind that the real question is process. Policy is your friend. In looking at a grade appeal, I don't ask whether I would have graded the assignment differently; that's not what an appeal should be about. Faculty should be given tremendous deference in their professional judgment of student work in the faculty's field of expertise; that's what they're hired to do. Appeals should be restricted to provable errors (such as data entry errors inputting the grades, or arithmetic errors in calculating them) or differential treatment. If Professor Jones is a hard grader, then she's a hard grader; that's part of academic freedom. If Professor Jones has a provable pattern of giving higher grades to handsome young men, then we have an entirely different (and actionable) issue.

From experience, I've also learned that student accusations against faculty are often based on extremely selective memory and a fair bit of embellishment. Heaven help the dean who takes a student's account uncritically.

Academic leadership sometimes means being the bad guy and telling the frustrated student that yes, she worked hard, but no, that doesn't count. Not every student succeeds at every task. I'd be worried about the mental health of anyone who enjoyed delivering that news, but sometimes it needs to be delivered. It comes with the job.

The Reality of Shared Governance

Woe betide the dean who thinks herself a manager in the traditional sense. Although certain deanly functions, such as evaluation, are consistent with traditional management roles, academia also has a contested but prized tradition of shared governance that complicates the picture.

Like "academic freedom," the concept of shared governance is both important and markedly elastic. As a rhetorical device, it's usually used in the service of whatever a given speaker wants, whether or not that use is consistent with prior or generally accepted uses. It's part of the cultural catechism, and as such it's widely recognized but often misunderstood.

Back when the faculty were the college, the idea of shared governance was relatively straightforward: the faculty would run the college as a committee of the whole, only occasionally delegating authority over dreary operational issues to administrators, who were understood to be something like secretaries. If you push some faculty advocates of shared governance into a corner, you'll find that they still think this way.

Of course, the faculty aren't the entire college anymore, and haven't been for a long time. Colleges are run by boards of trustees, who delegate authority to administrators. Colleges are accountable to all manner of external authority over which they lack veto power: federal, state, and local laws; funding requirements; donors; threats of litigation; administrative agencies and regulations; ever-evolving case law; students; and public opinion, for starters. And faculty aren't the only employees of the college, either; in addition to the loathed but necessary administrators, there's also a growing rank of full-time staff ranging from counselors to financial aid officers to building maintainers.

Although advocates of traditional shared governance tend to think of it as faculty governance, I have yet to identify a principled argument for why faculty should have a strong voice in governance and staff should not. On many campuses, tension persists between the two groups, based on everything from different schedules (most staff members work forty hours a week in the office, twelve months a year, and many have some choice words about faculty schedules), to perceived faculty arrogance, to tenure, to faculty resentment over staff resources. When faculty firebrands rail against "noninstructional" expenses in the budget, many staffers connect the dots pretty quickly.

These tensions can sound petty, and sometimes they are. But they become major issues when you actually try to get things done. Even such banalities as the scheduling of meetings can become contested. Is it fair to have task forces meet during the summer? Alternately, is it fair to expect the entire college to stop and sit on its hands all summer?

There's also the delicate issue of definition. Among whom is this governance shared? And governance of what, exactly?

Although some like to hold on to the centuries-old definition, a more realistic (though still flawed) understanding has emerged more recently. In this understanding, the faculty have unique say over curriculum and academic standards, while the administration handles the budget and related matters. This means that changes to programs—introductions of new programs, phasing out of existing programs, or significant changes to the composition of programs—should be run through the faculty in some sort of formal way. Meanwhile, the administration has say over tuition levels, facilities, and operational concerns.

Of course, the line isn't as clean as that. Faculty are paid, and programs require faculty. So does the decision to start a new program rest with faculty or administration? Alternately, when money is tight, does the decision to discontinue a program and lay off its faculty rest with faculty or with administration?[2]

Governance on the Ground

If you want to make an experienced academic groan, just mention the words "curriculum committee." Anyone who has endured curriculum committee deliberations knows how painful the discussions are, and how quickly talk of curriculum shades into discussion of resources. That's especially true when certain departments have capital or staff costs that go far beyond simply paying for the instructor. In a program like nursing, for example, it's common to have to pay for lab technicians, simulators, simulator technicians, and all manner of "consumables," in addition to paying premium rates for faculty and running small class sizes. The folks over in psychology have to overproduce to make up the difference. When the two groups are in the same union, the issues can get sticky.

At the community college level, of course, the external constraints on curriculum are also manifold, even if nobody wants to admit it. In the case of transfer-oriented programs, considerations of what the four-year schools will actually accept in transfer often trump local preferences. Programs with specific accreditations (such as nursing) often have specific requirements to maintain those accreditations. Some states have mandates for the general education block for a degree, so any degree has to include, say, English Comp 1 and 2. Many states also have maximum numbers of credits that an associate's degree can require. So when you start with the mandated gen ed block as the floor and the statewide credit cap as the ceiling, and then add transfer and accreditation considerations, the actual room to maneuver is often quite small. That's what makes curricular changes so wrenching. In most programs, adding one requirement means dropping another, and you can expect pushback from whoever is having his requirement dropped. I'm constantly struck by how quickly the discussions will move from high-minded invocations of academic integrity and excellence to outright horse-trading.

Finally, there's the basic contradiction between the ideal of shared governance as a sort of workers' cooperative and the fact that actual legal authority rests with the board of trustees and its designees in the administration. Even the stronger partisans of shared governance will usually concede, if pushed, that the senate is ultimately "advisory" to the president or board, and that the president or board (or both) has final say. However, in practice, failure to take the "advice" is usually viewed as a grave offense, and often leads to votes of no confidence.

Luckily, though, I've found that the majority of faculty care less about shared governance per se than they care about feeling respected and heard. The institutional mechanism is less important than the spirit animating it. That said, if an institutional mechanism doesn't exist, you'd be well advised to develop one. Even the gesture of establishing a venue for discussion will send a message.

Assuming the venue does exist, I'd advise using it for formative discussions, as well as for judgments of finished proposals. Given limited resources, we frequently make choices based on what's least bad, rather than what's ideal. But if you weren't privy to the process of winnowing down the options, all you see is the least-bad proposal, which, by itself, doesn't inspire confidence. When people walk through the formative process with you, though, they can see why the knee-jerk "Why don't we just . . .?" options aren't actually better or even possible. And of course, more eyes on the project in the early stages can sometimes generate real improvements, as those other eyes will see from angles that you won't.

Thomas Jefferson once wrote that the tree of liberty needs to be watered with the blood of revolution every twenty years or so. In my observation, that's also true of the venues for shared governance. On many campuses, these venues have long since been captured by a superannuated group of true believers who use it for their own purposes. What was supposed to be a source of open and candid debate has instead become a restrictive club open only to what Jeff Angus (2006) calls BITGODs ("Back in the Good Old Days . . ."). When the BITGODs have tenure and outsized personalities, they can poison the climate for everyone.

It's important to keep in mind the distinction between venue and spirit. If a given venue has become so encrusted with petty history as to defeat the larger purpose, it may be time to invent a new venue. This may have to happen on a fairly regular basis. The key here is not to make the mistake of attacking the old one first. You won't beat "something" with "nothing." Start by developing a new one in parallel, then just pay more attention to the new one than to the old one. A direct attack on the old one, in the absence of an alternative, will just look like an attack on the very idea of shared governance. Shared governance suffers if a small group captures the microphone forever; saving the spirit of shared governance may mean setting up a new microphone before taking down the old one.

Obviously, the BITGODs will push back, and you need to account for that. But if you can keep in mind that most of the time, the BITGODs' noise will far exceed their actual numbers, you may be able to isolate them over time. If you can find some reasonable consolation prize for them, something that plays to their strengths and sense of self-importance, you may actually wind up making nearly everybody happier. For instance, in my experience, BITGODs love to be involved in, say, graduation planning. The pomp and tradition appeal to them. In that setting, they can play to their strengths and still perform a meaningful service to the college.

4

HERDING CATS

MANAGING CREATIVE PEOPLE

PROBABLY THE SINGLE GREATEST OBSTACLE DEANS FACE is role ambiguity. What, exactly, should a dean do?

The ambiguity of the dean's role is really symptomatic of a larger ambiguity about academic roles. For example, many traditional faculty hold two conflicting points of view on "shared governance" simultaneously, though they fail to note the contradiction:

> *Nothing should be done on campus without the active participation and consent, if not enthusiasm, of the faculty.*
>
> *Faculty should be left alone at all times.*

It's possible to honor either of these, but simply impossible to honor both—assuming you do anything at all. The former position derives from the idea that the faculty is the college; this view is a holdover from medieval times, and though it's often presented as a version of workplace democracy, it's really rooted in an aristocratic conception of power. (To see that demonstrated, watch what happens when you try to define shared governance to include the maintenance staff or the students.) The latter position derives from the twentieth-century idea that faculty are essentially independent contractors on loan from their scholarly disciplines.[1] In this view, faculty's real attention is directed toward their own disciplinary associations; their employers are merely the folks who write the checks.

The dean's challenge lies in running the gauntlet between these two conflicting notions while accomplishing the job at hand. No small feat.

In this chapter, I outline some relatively common issues related to managing independent and creative people within the confines of a slow-moving organization, along with some recommendations for doing so.

Working with Faculty

Although colleges sell credentials, the quality of those credentials depends on the semiorganized efforts of intelligent and creative people who have their own, sometimes conflicting, agendas. Ensuring this quality entails providing enough direction and consistency that the college doesn't give in to its entropic tendencies, but not so much that creative people feel devalued or squelched. A sense of powerlessness or irrelevance can lead quickly to burnout. When someone with life tenure burns out decades before retirement, the college has a serious problem on its hands. Yet the realities of organizational life dictate that you can't just say yes to every request. What to do?

Context matters, obviously, but I've had good luck with a few approaches.

Assume the Best

One of my key strategies is to assume good faith, no matter how bizarre the initial assertion. Because no matter how weird their statements may sound, even people who are well off the mark generally think they're right. Until you figure out how they got there, you won't be able to reach them.

A year or so into my first deanship, I discovered the value of this approach. A high-performing but somewhat dramatic professor burst into my office, declaring loudly and vigorously that the evening dean was a liar and a rat, and that she refused to work with him anymore.

I knew both the professor and the evening dean, and thought well of them both. As far as I was concerned, this came out of the clear blue sky.

I asked her why she said that. When she caught her breath, she said that she had asked him a few weeks before about a potential course substitution for a few of her students, so they could graduate on time. (The course they normally would have needed wasn't offered that semester.) He had told her it was possible, so she passed that message on to the students. Then, the night before she met with me, the dean told her that the students didn't have what they needed and couldn't graduate. When she told him that he had approved the course substitution a few weeks prior, he denied having done that, and let her know that he resented her implication. Now she was fit to be tied, and the students were left hanging.

I told her I'd look into it.

Later that day, when the evening dean came in, I asked him why the professor was so mad at him. He immediately responded that he was mad at her, and that she was an unprofessional jerk who ran around slandering his good name.

After he vented for a bit, I asked him for his recollection of the story.

He recalled the earlier meeting with her. By his telling, she had asked if he could approve a course substitution for a few of her students. He didn't know, and said he'd look into it. I asked if he remembered exactly what he had said. He replied that he told her "It's *possible* . . . ," in the same tone of voice in which one would say "Maybe . . ."

Eureka!

In a way, they were both right. The professor was correct, technically, when she accused him of going from yes to no, because she heard "It's possible" as yes. But he didn't mean yes when he said it, so he was also right when he took offense at being called a liar. As far as he was concerned, he had told her he'd look into it, he did, and she went nuts.

Once I pieced that together, it became clear that the problem was actually a misunderstanding. The professor, acting in good faith, believed that she had been lied to. The evening dean, also acting in good faith, believed that he had been falsely accused. And both were emotional about it because they were both emotionally invested in their work and in doing a good job; both felt that they were being put in impossible, and undeserved, positions.

At that point, I spoke to each of them separately, walking them through the chronology as I understood it. After it seemed clear that each of them saw the misunderstanding, I asked them to speak to each other. They eventually did—I wasn't there—and decided that they could accept that neither was actually evil or incompetent. They found another solution for the students, and we were able to work together.

In some ways, this was a simple case of crossed wires. But the key moment involved stepping back from the initial conflict and trying to piece together how it could be that two well-meaning, intelligent people could butt heads like that. Rather than defaulting to "So-and-so is horrible," I assumed goodwill up front, leaving an opening for a solution in which everybody still felt valid and respected. Better, it set a precedent for dealing with similar issues in the future.

Know When to Listen, When to Share, and When to Keep a Secret

I've also found that playing the long game helps. If you sit in the dean's office long enough, you'll soon detect a pattern of people asking for quick-and-dirty interventions to solve particular problems. Most of the time, the intervention will seem like a reasonable answer to the particular situation, considered in a vacuum. But the savvy dean will be aware of what it means to set a precedent, and how other people will interpret any interventions.

Professor Jones doesn't want any classes after 2:00, so she can be home when her kid comes home from school. Professor Smith doesn't want Professor Jones to get any special treatment, as Smith feels undervalued and thinks that Jones is overvalued. The schedule aligns in such a way that it's possible to give Jones what she wants, but not without making it obvious.

Scheduling is thorny enough without issues of special treatment entering into the equation. When they do, it's important to know what you're dealing with.

Whenever possible, it's best to come up with some sort of publicly acceptable explanation for the decisions you made, and then to share it. As I've noted elsewhere, angry people will fill information vacuums with theories of their own, and the invented answers will usually be much more sinister than the truth. To the extent that you can get everyone's cards on the table, it will be easier to resolve the conflicts in ways that don't leave anyone unnecessarily embittered.

One way to do that is to find out why people want the time slots they want. Sometimes it's possible to satisfy the actual motivating desire through another method. Do you want the Tuesday–Thursday 11:00 slot because it always runs, or because you have another commitment at another time, or because you'll be damned if that prima donna gets it again? Knowing which of those—or something else—is behind the request can make it easier to settle.

Finding answers that way is all the more important because sometimes you can't. And when you're stuck, you need to have a reservoir of trust built up. The bane of the administrator's existence is being caught between what looks like favoritism and the realities of confidentiality.

For example, at one job, I had a professor who had a serious medical condition he didn't want to become public knowledge. His condition made it difficult for him to take early morning classes, though he was fine with late afternoons. After a couple semesters of that, rumors started to fly that he got his first preferences because of . . . well, there had to be something sinister.

There wasn't, but I just couldn't betray the confidence and explain it. So I did what I could, which was to call a couple of the louder complainers in individually, remind them of how well they were treated generally, and then just say that there were valid reasons that I simply could not share, and that I needed them to trust me to be telling the truth.

I can't say it was an easy sell, and I don't know if they actually believed me or not, but I had enough credibility with them at that point that the complaining subsided. Sometimes the best you can do is get to "Well, I'm sure he has his reasons." This is not ideal, but sometimes it's the best available option. It's best to make that option available in advance by building trust over time, so that when you need it, it's there.

Know the Difference Between Power and Control—and Which Matters

Sometimes you have a faculty that wants power with no responsibility, and a dean who has responsibility with little real power. It's easy to lose heart in a setting like that.

What you need to understand is the crucial difference between power and control. You can increase your power—that is, your effectiveness— by giving up control.

I've read plenty of management books aimed at corporate managers, but the usual management techniques seldom apply in my job. For example, you can't just weed out the troublemakers as a way to manage conflict. Given that most of the time, college administrators are stuck with their tenured faculty, how does one handle conflict in productive (or at least minimally destructive) ways?

One key method is to focus on process, rather than on content or result. Before deciding who is right or wrong, decide how you're going to go about deciding. Too many people skip this step and go directly to trying to find the right answer. Big mistake.

If you make decisions on what I'll call a personalistic basis—based on personal likes or dislikes, hunches, gut feelings, or whatever euphemism for "arbitrarily" you prefer—you will teach people that the way to get what they want is to distort your perceptions. You will rapidly divert the energy of the organization away from the work at hand and toward feeding you a steady diet of lies. Sooner or later, you'll make a truly awful decision based on bad information, and the house of cards will come tumbling down. (From the organization's perspective, the personalistic style guarantees turmoil whenever there's turnover. Given the speed of administrative turnover in many places, this is no small thing.)

Alternately, if you decide based on conflict avoidance, you will paradoxically ratchet up the level of conflict. Once people figure out that you will appease the one who shouts the loudest, you will be barraged with shouting. Incentives matter.

If you decide based entirely on mechanistic numerical formulae, expect extended hair-splitting arguments about data and really tiresome orations about the ineffable (whatever) that isn't captured in your numbers.

But if you spend most of your energy setting up venues and protocols for groups to make decisions, and you signal your willingness to abide by the reasonable decisions of the group even when they aren't what you personally would have done, you'll be in much better shape.

Practice Humility

If you start from the correct assumption that a whole cluster of very intelligent people is smarter collectively than you are individually, then it makes sense to try to engineer ways in which you can harness that collective intelligence. That means giving it just enough direction so that it addresses the right problems; providing some resources—usually time, but sometimes money—so that folks can spend time meeting and discussing; and being willing to defer strongly to whatever the group finally decides.

For example, much of the recent literature on student success in developmental courses shows that the longer the sequence, the fewer the students who will succeed (Edgecombe, 2011). In a way, that's counterintuitive for many academics, as we tend to use a deficit model in thinking about remediation. If two semesters of remediation lead to poor results, they must not be enough—let's do three! But in fact, the longer the sequence takes, the more time there is for life to get in the way. Further, students are demoralized when faced with the prospect of over a year's worth of courses that don't count for graduation.

When I arrived, my college was no different from most. It had a three-semester developmental math sequence, and there was serious talk—in which I participated—of adding a fourth, on the theory that some students weren't even strong enough upon arrival to handle the basic arithmetic class.

By happy coincidence, I learned about the Community College Research Center studies on developmental sequences just before the state put out a Request for Proposals for projects to improve student success rates in developmental math. So I went to the math department and offered a deal. I would use the grant to give the department several course releases and some travel money to be shared among the full-time faculty. In return, they would use that time and money to explore and develop a shorter developmental sequence, with the goal of running the new sequence the following year. They took the deal.

The strategy worked, because it hit a whole series of right notes. It recognized, in a really fundamental way, that course content and course design are properly the province of faculty. And although I set the goal of "Get them to college math faster," I didn't tell them how to achieve that goal. Every decision about hours, content, order, and materials was theirs. When they presented their solutions, I happily deferred to them. I committed up front to honoring their findings, and followed through on my commitment. As a result, they didn't get the demoralizing sense that what they did wouldn't matter.

It also recognized that innovation takes time and resources. Requests for extra work without extra compensation—whether in the form of extra money or in of having other work taken off their plates—tend to fall flat, and with understandable reason. But having a course taken off their schedules opened up time to have meetings and go on field trips to other colleges that had similar goals and were trying various methods to achieve them.

Stick to Roles and Rules

Discussing roles and rules, rather than personal motives, can allow people to save face even as they retreat. This matters more than one might expect.

The more emotionally charged the issue, the more the roles-and-rules strategy can help. For example, when allegations of bias are on the table—based on race, gender, age, sexual orientation, or whatever— the accused often feels that her personal integrity has been brought into question. That tends to lead to defensiveness and escalation of countercharges; before long, you're caught in a spiral of silliness.

Moving the discussion away from "motive" and toward actions and procedures has a double benefit. It prevents undue psychologizing and defensive posturing, and it actually offers a chance to both solve the immediate problem and prevent the next one. It's impossible to know what's in someone's heart, and at some level, it's a little creepy to try. Better to address what can be addressed, which is observable behavior.

For example, in a faculty search committee I was on about ten years ago, one leading candidate was a very masculine lesbian. In deliberations, a senior member of the committee suggested that the candidate might not be comfortable there, given the rough edges many of the students had. I didn't know if the concerns were genuine or a cover for her own discomfort, but it sounded discriminatory to me. I responded by suggesting that we should probably leave the question of her own comfort to the candidate herself, as it's always hard to know who will work out and who won't. The suggestion went over well, because the senior member wasn't accused of anything and didn't have to defend herself in order to retreat gracefully.

Keep a Tight Hand on the Reins—Dealing with Victim Bullies

Of course, at bottom, managing people means dealing with personalities.

In her glorious and invaluable *The College Administrator's Survival Guide*, C. K. Gunsalus (2006) coins the term "victim bullies" to describe employees—usually tenured faculty—who use claims of victimization as weapons. These people combine narcissism, legal nitpicking, and extreme tendentiousness, and they usually wind up getting what they want. They're remarkably common in academic settings, which value both relative independence and strong verbal skills. Handling these folks is a serious challenge.

In my experience, victim bullies usually seize on whatever protected class membership they can claim—race, gender, age, sexual orientation, whatever is at hand—and ascribe any no they receive to an agenda against their protected class. ("You're only saying that because I'm black/female/young/old/gay/fill in the blank!") Worse, because victim bullies are really more narcissistic than political, they play those cards opportunistically rather than ethically. Reciprocity is the foundation of ethical behavior, and their narcissism precludes reciprocity; at a really basic level, they simply don't see other people as meaningful. They will recruit and discard allies as needed, with no regard for the damage done.

Part of what makes victim bullies as tiresome as they are is that they don't accept defeat. They just grind, grind, grind at their cause until someone appeases them to make them go away. Over time, they manage to escape meaningful supervision, just because nobody has the patience to deal with them for very long; they are simply more trouble than they're worth.

(One tip I've learned the hard way: when you get the hate-o-gram from the victim bully—usually several single-spaced pages, rife with cascading accusations—avoid the temptation to fire off a point-by-point rebuttal. Stick with calm language, address the minimum possible, and steer toward process. Just as bloggers are advised not to feed trolls, deans are advised not to respond tit-for-tat to victim bullies. It only encourages them.)

In a rational organization, victim bullies would simply be fired. As Robert Sutton (2007) documented in *The No Asshole Rule*, a single toxic personality can bring down the performance of a dozen others around him. Within academia, the lip service paid to "collegiality" is supposed to address this at some level, but firing someone with tenure for lack of collegiality is effectively impossible. It's lawsuit bait. Given the looseness with which "academic freedom" is typically defined, one can hide all manner of sins within it. Once a victim bully is tenured, the best strategy for a dean to use is containment.

Containment requires working on two fronts. The first is documentation. Rigorous documentation of the reasons for saying no can prevent legal trouble later. Careful documentation of every incident of inappropriate behavior and every false charge can lay a paper trail that you may need later.

The second is self-control. No matter how maddening the charges and behavior, the dean should not respond in kind, nor should she effectively reward tantrums by appeasing them. Part of what makes victim bullies as tenacious as they are is their occasional success. No matter how tempting it may be to solve the short-term problem through appeasement, it's crucial to remember that incentives matter. If tantrums and spurious charges are rewarded, expect more of them. If they get nowhere, but constructive dialogue succeeds instead, then those who are capable of either will make the constructive choice. Over time, the victim bullies will become more isolated and less relevant.

This is all easier said than done, of course, especially when charges that can be couched in terms of civil rights are given automatic deference. But it's the only way to stop the madness.

Be Straight with Exiles

Many community college faculty never intended to be community college faculty. They originally expected to work in the type of universities they attended for graduate school, or perhaps the small liberal arts colleges where many of them did their undergraduate work. When the academic job market didn't agree, they took the jobs they could get.

Many of them make the adjustment relatively well. But some, unfortunately, never really come to terms with where they've landed. The lack of prestige gnaws at them, and the large teaching loads and limited time for research frustrate them. Over time, these people can become remarkably crabby, often lashing out at trivial provocations.

The best strategy I've found for coping with those who feel like exiles—as I did at FPU—is simply to be truthful about what the college can and cannot do. As with victim bullies, apologies and appeasement simply won't work; no matter how you slice it, a five-course-per-semester teaching load with developmental students is not the same as a two-course load of junior and senior majors. Well-intended efforts at glossing over the difference will actually just stir greater disappointment over time, as the gap between what a community college is and what they want it to be simply gets clearer.

Some exiles will gradually get over it. Some will find ways other than research to make a mark in the world, such as through administration. But some just can't let go of the dream of teaching at Oberlin.

When I moved into administration at FPU, one of my first challenges was a gifted professor (and a personal friend) whose bitterness at being at FPU was conspicuously getting the better of him. In his mind, he belonged at Yale, and anything else was just a daily slap in the face. Although his teaching remained outstanding, he became progressively more hostile and bitter to his colleagues.

In the midst of one of many discussions we had about the unfairness of the universe, I had a moment of inspiration and offered him a deal. If he would stop the grandstanding and just do his job well, I would write him the most glowing reference he could possibly want, and would approve any time off he needed for job interviews, without question. In essence, I offered to help him get what he really wanted, which was "out."

It worked. For the rest of that year, he taught well and otherwise minded his own business. I gave him a reference that accurately reflected his real gifts as a teacher, without any negativity about the rest of it. I even coached him on interview tactics. At the end of the year, an offer from a traditional college came through, and he left with a smile. He landed someplace where he could be happy, FPU got a good year out of him, and he stopped poisoning the well. Some exiles simply have to go home to be happy; it's best for all involved if they're encouraged.

Don't Try to Mix Oil and Water

Sometimes, of course, the conflict is interpersonal and not really based on something that can be addressed by group deliberation. Sometimes Professor Hatfield and Professor McCoy just don't like each other, and have built a long and storied history of unpleasantness.

Rather than getting involved at the detail level and trying to suss out who's right—typically, they're both at least slightly wrong—it's typically more productive to draw a distinction between colleagues and friends. Nobody has to be anybody's friend against his will, and it's important to respect that. However, working together doesn't require being friends. It just requires enough mutual acknowledgment to allow the work to get done. If you can get to that level, call it good and move on.

Hiring, Firing, and Promotions

Bureaucracy is built to handle routine and mindless tasks, but the work of teaching is inherently creative, and the people who are drawn to it tend to be both creative and highly intelligent. In other words, for reasons good and bad, they're constantly spilling outside the lines.

In a public system, the lines are often quite numerous and sometimes overlapping. Overlay federal, state, and local laws and policies with collective bargaining agreements, "past practices," grant rules, affirmative action and nondiscrimination policies, grievance settlements, and political realities, and you wind up with a dense and incoherent lattice in which to move. Combine a remarkably thick patchwork of rules with an uncommonly creative and independent-minded workforce, and you have a serious management challenge. Add chronic, serious, and increasing resource constraints, and you start to understand the turnover rate in academic administration.

Much of the management literature aimed at the private sector is of little to no use in this context. I've had to smile when reading Jim Collins's admonitions (2001) that it's all about getting the right people on the bus, for example. Well, yes, that would be nice, but if you inherit a bunch of people who got tenure decades ago, that doesn't help you. They're on the bus, and they're not moving.[2] Jack Welch's idea of just dismissing the bottom 10 percent every few years is similarly otherworldly. Even if you could somehow identify the bottom 10 percent of your faculty—and good luck doing that in a way that would stand up to the inevitable legal challenges—low performance simply doesn't rise to the level of "cause" necessary to dismiss someone with tenure.

Manipulating incentives is similarly difficult when promotion and tenure guidelines are collectively bargained. "Attaboys" go only so far when dealing with contrarian and highly intelligent people. So what's a dean to do?

Faculty Turnover—or Lack Thereof

After the building boom of the 1960s, community college faculty hiring slowed dramatically. That's particularly true in the evergreen disciplines, as those were usually the first things to get staffed, and those are the faculty with the fewest nonacademic options.

I saw this most dramatically at my first community college. When I arrived as dean, I was thirty-four; the median age of the full-time faculty was sixty. (I actually checked.) The vast majority had been hired within the first ten years of the college's existence, with a smaller wave following in the mid-1980s; since then, hires had been few and far between.[3]

The generational pattern was especially striking when compared to the staff. Staff had turned over in a more normal pattern over the years, so when I got there, much of the staff was considerably younger than most of the faculty.

The college had a tenure system, the faculty union contract rewarded seniority above all else, and there was no mandatory retirement age, so compensation was entirely disconnected from performance. People were open and even smug about riding out the clock.

The intersection of the pig-in-a-python staffing pattern with the rise of affirmative action meant that on the rare occasions when new "lines" did come along, they were hotly contested. Unfortunately, that often meant that the new kid was also an awkward cultural fit, and real tensions arose around that. What little faculty turnover that did exist often consisted of women of color leaving for more appealing offers.

Because so many faculty had been playing in the same sandbox for far too long, new questions or issues were invariably read in light of much older ones. It took me several years to start to parse the code. When Professor Smith referred obsessively to "academic integrity," she was really taking a shot at Professor Jones, who typically responded with a glancing reference to a long-gone colleague the first one disliked. The layers of implication were thick and sedimentary, making constructive dialogue much harder than it needed to be.

I was also struck by the consequences for the college as a whole when too many faculty are concentrated at the same stage of the life cycle. When you have too many rookies, you get lots of rookie mistakes. When you have too many riding out the clock, you get many variations on "No thanks, I've paid my dues" whenever something comes along. When entire departments feel as though they've paid their dues and they'd rather just be left alone to fatten up their pensions, it can be difficult to make progress on the issues at hand.

I noticed this phenomenon in regard to assessment of general education. When I raised the issue, around 2006, I was told "Oh, we did that back in '96," as if that answered the question. New issues would be greeted with rolled eyes and variations on "Ugh, not that again . . ."

Coming to grips with current needs often required coming to grips with the ghosts of conflicts past.

Finding Buried Treasure

Although "diversity" has been recognized legally as a valid reason for preferential hiring along racial or gender lines, it has not been recognized for age; if your median age is sixty, you aren't legally allowed to try to diversify by generation. That's a hole in the law, but I don't expect it to change anytime soon, given the higher voting rates of older people and the average ages of members of Congress and the judicial branch. Trying consciously to diversify your workforce by generation would still be considered age discrimination, even though doing something analogous for race or gender would be considered affirmative action.

In a system with tenure and unions, it's incredibly difficult to balance a top-heavy faculty. In the past, some states or systems tried early retirement incentives, but those have fallen out of favor as states did the math and realized that they lost money on the deal. Because there's no automatic "out" anymore—it was age seventy until 1994—you have to wait until people choose to go.

As mentioned earlier, some administrators will try to force the issue by making life progressively more unpleasant for the people they'd rather be rid of, until they get the hint and go. There are ways of doing that—giving undesirable schedules, say, or being generally unpleasant—but they're extremely high cost politically, and often legally. People who might not lift a finger to help with student advising or outcomes assessment will often have the union rep on speed-dial. They also have friends, and some folks who don't know the whole story will rally to their side out of fear of precedent. Getting into a war of attrition with somebody who has tenure and a union is generally a losing proposition, even if you have the facts on your side.

As real as the issues of generational diversity are, though, they're largely beyond the power of any one dean to change. Addressing generational diversity effectively would require the law to shift in ways that don't seem likely.

On the upside, though, sometimes you can find "buried treasure" among your senior faculty. At two different colleges, I've found senior faculty who had been exiled to the margins of their departments years before I arrived, for offenses nobody could quite remember or that no longer seemed relevant. In the time I had worked with them, they struck me as much more capable than their treatment suggested. When the right opportunities came along, I asked them if they'd be willing to return to a sort of prominence and take on central roles; both happily agreed, and both performed admirably. Watching some talented but long-neglected faculty come into their own again was gratifying, and was a much better use of resources than just paying high salaries for people to sit on the sidelines. It also improved morale in some corners, as the friends of the long-ignored faculty saw some old wrongs righted. If you have the chance to do something like this, I really can't recommend it highly enough.

Incentives and Service

I sometimes think that economics for laypeople can be boiled down to two phrases: "supply and demand" and "incentives matter." Most people have a decent grasp of the former, but are shaky at best on the latter. Administrators ignore incentives at their peril.

In the research university world, talk of perverse incentives usually refers to the common practice of hiring people to teach, then firing them for not doing enough research. The savvier faculty figure out quickly that research is the name of the game, and direct their energies accordingly; when students complain that the professors don't give them much thought, the professors simply point to the internal reward structure. If you want teaching, they say, pay for it.

In the community college world, there's a similar (if less dramatic) dynamic around college service. Faculty workloads usually include a service component, defined typically as serving on various committees, but the same faces keep popping up over and over again. (Put differently, some people manage to dodge any meaningful committee work for years at a time, and even brag about it.) When pressed, they point out that their salary and promotion prospects are generally unaffected by service. If you want service, they suggest, pay for it.

Of course, "pay for it" is a trap. Once you start paying extra for one thing, you implicitly devalue everything else you aren't paying for yet. And it has never been clear to me how the same people who argue that tenure is necessary to preserve faculty control over the college also simultaneously argue that committee work is an undue burden. It's one or the other. Either faculty get tenure precisely because they're professionals who can be expected to go above and beyond—and therefore shouldn't get extra pay for service—or they're pieceworkers who should get paid by the unit of work, whether teaching or service. Of course, if it's the latter, then the argument for tenure collapses.

But on the ground, many faculty are utterly unbothered by the contradiction. As an administrator, you will frequently find yourself in the position of trying to get people to do things for which the short-term payoff to them is zero or negative.

When possible, of course, the ideal solution is to align the incentives with the desired outcomes. Just be careful not to overshoot. For example, although it's nice to have student evaluations reflect well on the faculty, placing too much weight on student evaluations can lead nervous professors to "game" the system by giving easier grades or picking a strategic day for handing out evaluations or just emphasizing the more entertaining side of teaching. Similarly, although it would be irresponsible to completely ignore pass rates, placing too much weight on them will lead professors to lower their standards.

A wise dean will know—and communicate—that some level of student failure and student crankiness is simply a sign that the professor is doing her job. Similarly, not all dissatisfaction should be treated equally. When looking at student evaluations, a few comments to the effect that "she grades too hard" or that "there's too much homework" should be expected, and not held against anybody. But if you get a raft of comments along the line of "She takes two months to return papers" or "She cancels class a lot," it's fair to ask some questions.

Adjunct Instructors: The Fuel in the Community College Engine

The other half of the faculty turnover equation, of course, is the shift from full-timers to adjuncts. In many ways, I see this as the logical consequence of the extreme security of the tenured. The institutional risk that would normally be borne by all employees has been distributed asymmetrically; the risk that tenured faculty are spared is shifted onto the backs of the adjunct faculty. A more equitable distribution of risk would mean a fairer deal for the people who are now adjuncts and a fairer deal for students, considering that many of their teachers are currently effectively unaccountable for their performance.

Across the country, the majority of credit hours taught at community colleges are taught by adjuncts. Although some people like to imagine that this was the result of a conscious, decades-long conspiracy by academic administrators to circumvent the power of the faculty, it was really the logical, if unintended, consequence of the intersection of budget constraints with absolute inflexibility on the tenured side.

The primary advantage to colleges of going the adjunct route is cost. Adjuncts generally are paid by the credit hour or by the course, with few or no benefits. Because benefit costs—especially health insurance—are rising far faster than inflation or appropriations, increasing the number of people who don't receive them helps bend the cost curve.

The original idea behind the adjunct category was that adjuncts were employed elsewhere full-time and just teaching on the side—the practicing attorney who picks up a night class, say—or were educated stay-at-home spouses (usually wives) who liked to stretch their minds and pick up a few bucks without taking on the burden of a full-time job. Both of those categories actually exist, even now; at my first community college, which was located in a very affluent area, we had a surprising number of executives' wives among the adjuncts. The low pay and lack of benefits weren't deal-breakers for them, as they were already covered at home. Better, some of them stuck around for years at a time, doing wonderful work in the classroom at low cost.

Depending on location, some colleges also draw on local graduate students as adjuncts. In those cases, the implied trade is low pay in exchange for gaining experience. Universities have long run this model, using graduate students as teaching assistants for undergraduate sections; now, many colleges within driving distance of universities draw on that same pool for adjuncts. The upside for the college is that you get enthusiastic, recently trained people at low cost. The downsides are that they're inexperienced and typically just passing through.

Adjuncting also works fairly well for artists or musicians or others who have sporadic work schedules and like something fairly steady on the side to help them get through the dry spells. For musicians in particular, who usually work at night, picking up a day class can be a nice way to earn some money on the side without interfering with their vocation. Because very few colleges could ever afford to hire a separate full-time person for every instrument, having some adjuncts around makes it possible to fill out the offerings without busting the budget.

Finally, of course, adjuncts help colleges deal with enrollment fluctuations and staff emergencies. In the Great Recession of 2009, my college broke its previous enrollment record by a thousand students, even while taking midyear budget cuts from the state; if not for adjuncts, it would have had to turn away students at the moment of their greatest need. Adjuncts also come in handy for abrupt medical emergencies, maternity leaves, and unexpected departures.

All of that said, though, it's still true that the use of adjuncts goes well beyond specialty courses, emergencies, and graduate student training. And the college's savings come at a direct cost—financial and often personal—to the adjuncts themselves. The term "freeway flier" describes an adjunct who tries to cobble together a living by teaching courses at several colleges simultaneously; what was once fairly unusual has now become common and even expected.

I've been a freeway flier myself. Shortly after graduating with my doctorate, I pieced together a semblance of a living for a while by driving among three different places, teaching SAT prep, English composition, and my social science discipline. It was crazymaking and remarkably low paying; I realized quickly that it was just enough to continue my graduate student lifestyle as long as the student loan grace period lasted and I didn't need any car repairs. In other words, it could tide me over for a few months, but it was nothing resembling an acceptable long-term solution.

Luckily for me, FPU was in expansion mode at the time, and my peculiar mix of disciplines fit its needs nicely. It treated my adjunct time there as an extended audition for a full-time job. It wasn't until years later that I realized how unusual that was, and how lucky I was.

The Plight of Freeway Fliers

From the outside, it can be difficult to understand why educated people—many with doctorates, and almost all with at least master's degrees—would willingly put themselves through years of insecure, low-paid, geographically scattered jobs in hopes of eventually landing somewhere that might pay them in the mid-$40s if they're lucky.

At one level, adjuncting is a way for people who love to teach to be able to, even while pursuing other careers. When a local attorney teaches a business law class at night mostly for the sheer joy of it, the low pay isn't much of an issue. Conversely, adjunct teaching is a way for many high school teachers to supplement their income and stretch their pedagogical wings. But these relatively unobjectionable circumstances are far from exhaustive.

Part of the draw is the perceived (and sometimes real) lack of alternative. The nonacademic world generally doesn't jump to hire English PhD's, and if you need money now, you need money now. Adjuncting doesn't pay much, but it pays quickly, and sometimes you can't afford to wait. (The same argument applies to full-time faculty who regularly teach "overloads" for extra pay. I've repeatedly seen faculty whose kids are in college pick up multiple overload courses to help with tuition until the last kid graduates, at which point they happily drop back to their regular load.)

But I'm increasingly convinced that much of the felt "path dependence" that leads to ongoing adjuncting is driven by the search for validation. By the time someone gets a doctorate in a liberal arts discipline, she has been a good student for a very long time. She has jumped through hoops successfully for decades, navigating the hazards of high school, college, and graduate school with distinction. Through graduate school, she has been inculcated in a value system that disparages the idea of working for money and implies that any life other than "the life of the mind"—which is usually understood to mean "a tenured professorship at an exclusive school"—represents failure.

Worse, the myth of meritocracy survives, even when a catastrophic job market would seem to suggest a certain implausibility. The myth of meritocracy does real damage. After all, if the job market reflects merit and you can't find a job, what does that say about you? At that point, a job is more than just a way to make a living, as important as that is; it's also a validation of the choices and sacrifices you've made throughout (and since) graduate school. Much of the bitterness on academic blogs stems from a sense of betrayal by the profession, grounded in a sense of entitlement violated.

Of course, the myth of meritocracy is exactly that. Job postings didn't drop by a third last year because the applicants suddenly got worse, but if you're an unsuccessful applicant, it's hard not to take rejection personally. (Obviously, the financial implications are personal.) When someone who has had nothing but academic success for decades on end runs headlong into this job market, a certain disbelief is understandable. "I just need one more year" becomes a mantra. Between denial, disbelief, and path dependence, smart people can find themselves on the treadmill for years at a time.

The freeway-flier lifestyle can do psychological damage that goes well beyond individual disappointment and a series of self-defeating decisions. It also poisons relationships.

When the two members of an academic couple are on the market at the same time, the "two-body" problem quickly rears its head. The academic job market is national, and good jobs are scarce. That means that anyone who's serious about finding a position has to be willing to move just about anywhere in the country for a job.

In the parlance of higher ed, if a couple moves for one person's job, the other person is the "trailing spouse" (or trailing partner). The trailing spouse situation isn't easy on any level.

Some colleges will try to create positions for the trailing spouse. That raises obvious issues of equity for other applicants—"Whom do I have to sleep with to get this job?" actually has an *answer*—as well as the prospect of having to spend rare resources on a suboptimal hire.

It also puts the trailing spouse in a difficult spot in terms of earning respect. If you come in already branded as a sort of consolation prize, it can be difficult to win respect in your own right.

Finally, of course, there's the sad fact that not all couples are forever. If the couple breaks up and the desirable half decamps for greener pastures, the college is stuck with the person it didn't really want in the first place. Alternately, if the trailing spouse does a terrible job, the college can be in the difficult position of either firing one while trying to hold on to the other—that tends to poison the well a bit—or tolerating low performance by one as the price of holding the other. If they're both in the same department, that's one thing, but if the trailing and failing spouse is in another department, you can expect that other department to complain mightily, and with some justification.

If the academic job market were more robust, the trailing-spouse issue would largely fade away. It's one thing to follow my wife if I'm confident that I can get a good job within easy commuting distance of where she is; it's something else altogether if I suspect that following her means tanking my career.

In my limited observation, colleges in isolated rural locations have typically been more accommodating of trailing spouses than colleges in more populated areas. That makes sense; alternative jobs are more plentiful in New York City than they are in, say, Plattsburgh. Getting someone to stay for an extended period in the middle of nowhere may require acknowledging the reality of couplehood in a way that getting someone to stay in Boston might not. Ultimately, of course, this is a much larger issue than any one college can solve.

Choosing Your Battles

In the end, managing creative people often involves drawing a distinction between what can be done and what's worth doing. If creative people are beaten down and demoralized, they will not do their best work. It is nearly always better to address the causes of frustration than to wait for a crisis and then hide behind legalisms, however correct they may be.

That said, solving the issues of moribund faculty, freeway fliers, and the like will take far more than just some consciousness raising or increased funding. At base, these are issues of structure. In Chapter Six, I'll suggest some possibilities for restructuring the academic hiring system to make it fairer, more humane, and more sustainable.

REGULAR CHALLENGES
OF THE DEAN'S JOB

ALTHOUGH LOCAL CONTEXT CERTAINLY MATTERS, the role of the dean—or of the midlevel academic manager—has some pretty common challenges. Money and resources are chronic issues, of course, as is managing faculty. Those have been addressed in earlier chapters. In this chapter, I take up other issues I have encountered, and offer, where possible, my thoughts on how best to handle them.

Surviving Administrative Turnover—or Not

Although the average length of term for a college president is seven years, the average length of term for a chief academic officer—typically the person to whom a dean reports—is only three to four years (Jaschik, 2007). That's one of those statistics that suggests a lot more than it says. Administrative turnover presents real challenges to the administrators who stick around.

New presidents frequently bring new administrative teams in with them, either immediately or shortly after arrival. Because presidents are often consumed largely with external relations—donors, political officials, community organizations, and local school districts, as well as the board of trustees—most of the internal issues fall to the vice presidents.[1] Consequently, the arrival of a new academic vice president can be a major change on campus.

When that major change happens every few years, the college can find it difficult to maintain a consistent direction over time. Each new VP has a different set of priorities, a different personal style, and a different management style. (The same is true with new deans, though their scope of control is much narrower.)

The savvy administrator will take pains to minimize the personalistic aspect of management. Succeeding someone who practiced the personalistic style takes time and patience, as so many decisions (and promises) have been based on factors that nobody wrote down and that many people will understand differently, if at all.

Turnover happens for a host of reasons. Given the average ages of higher-level administrators, a fair bit of it comes from retirements. Some comes from idiosyncratic personal considerations: family or spousal issues, an offer they couldn't refuse, or a long-running desire to return to the classroom. But there's also a special kind of frustration in these jobs that I suspect leads to much higher turnover than we might otherwise expect.

I have no data on this—it's not clear to me how one would even measure it—but I suspect that another major reason administrators leave is the need to present a united front, even when they personally disagree with a given policy or decision. Depending on the severity and frequency of dissonance, that can become a major stressor. This is especially true when administrators have to defend policies with which they disagree against attacks with which they agree. Representing a policy you don't believe in—especially under fire—is no fun.

As regrettable as that is, the alternative is hard to imagine. For a college to move in a particular direction consistently, the entire administration has to row in the same direction. A single dean making himself a public dissident becomes a distraction and can cause real harm. When that happens repeatedly, upper management will start to wonder, with some justification, what they're paying for.

The rule of thumb for dissent within administration is that the more private the setting, the more candid you can be. My boss and I have an agreement—as I've had with all of my bosses, and I do with my own direct reports—that in one-on-one meetings behind closed doors, arguments can be candid and even heated. In some small-group meetings, a slightly watered-down version of the same rule can hold. But once the discussion is over and the idea has gone from "proposal" to "announcement," the job at hand is to carry out the decision.

Everyone has to decide for herself the point at which the dissonance between "what I think" and "what I have to embody" becomes too great. For me, it happened fairly quickly at FPU; my solution was to find another job. FPU made a series of judgment calls I considered ill-advised and even self-defeating in my time there. None of them reached the level of illegality—I never felt like a whistleblower—they just struck me as wrongheaded. When I realized that they were all pointing in the same direction and that the direction had been set strongly from above, I decided it was time to go. If I couldn't row in the same direction as everyone else, I needed to join a new crew.

Making Transparency Work in Your Favor

Although certain personnel matters have to remain confidential, the savvy dean is well advised to assume that just about anything else could become public at any moment. Faculty talk to each other, and as anyone who has played Telephone as a kid knows, messages can get garbled in transmission.

Electronic communication has made an already porous environment much more so. Emails are forever, they can be forwarded to whomever, and they don't convey tone or context well. (Text messages are even worse, as they're far too short even to convey context.) Social media often blur the lines between professional and personal lives, which can lead to issues when people become inappropriately familiar. And considering the polarized politics of the external world, some enterprising demagogue could come along at any time and seize on something eyebrow raising to further some external agenda. ("Your tax dollars are paying full-time salaries to people who work only fifteen hours a week!")

Even if a dean manages to keep his side deals quiet, he will quickly find that faculty are intelligent and creative people and that they'll fill any "explanation gap" with theories of their own. Typically, the substitute explanations they generate will be far more disturbing and sinister than the truth, and they'll take "stonewalling" as confirmation. Every few months, I used to get some irate professor storming into my office connecting dots in really creative ways and using those constellations as evidence of my secret agenda to do something nefarious. Usually it was something that had never occurred to me; in a few cases, I actually laughed out loud before realizing what I was doing.

After a few years, I found that the best defense is a good offense. Rather than reacting to misunderstandings as they arose, I use the greater fluidity of electronic communication to put my arguments out there for public consumption and debate.

I've tried blogging for this purpose on my campus, and once the faculty got past their initial disbelief, it became a useful part of my repertoire. I've been able to crowdsource some difficult dilemmas and have benefited from suggestions that I wouldn't have received otherwise. Even better, when people are able to follow the logic behind a decision, they're able to "agree to disagree" with decisions they don't like, rather than ascribing them to base motives. The resulting improvement in the climate of campus civility has been to everyone's benefit: now we're able to discuss difficult issues simply by discussing them.

Of course, part of improving the climate of communication involves giving up the pretense of always being right. I've changed my own proposals when others have come along with better ideas or with compelling critiques that I simply hadn't thought of. Admitting "Gee, I hadn't thought of that" can be surprisingly disarming and can actually build your own credibility over time. And that is far more important than winning every point. If you can model the behavior you want to encourage—deferring to better ideas, say—you stand a better chance of seeing more of it.

Sometimes, of course, giving others a venue means hearing things you wish weren't true. The first time you kick some rocks over, ugly stuff will slither out. But pretending that stuff isn't there won't make it go away. As Hegel famously noted, "Freedom is the insight into necessity"; only by coming to grips with reality can we hope to make a real difference in it. And when people realize that they can ask difficult questions without being personally attacked or stigmatized, it becomes easier to make progress on those "everybody knows" dilemmas that typically go unaddressed for fear of ugly conflict.

When I arrived at my current college, for example, there was no "faculty only" venue for discussing academic issues. The College Senate (appropriately) comprised representatives from faculty, staff, and administration, and even the faculty union included full-time professional staff. (I never really understood the reason for that, and it led to all manner of intraunit tensions, but it wasn't my call.) During my interview, I asked one professor what the faculty were concerned about; he could only shrug and say that there was really no way of knowing. That didn't strike me as healthy or helpful.

Shortly after arriving, I worked with the faculty to establish a Faculty Council, reporting in an advisory capacity to the chief academic officer. After some initial clarifying of boundaries—deciding which issues were really union issues, which were College Senate, and which were Faculty Council—it quickly evolved into a constructive and useful venue for both feedback on concrete proposals and the formation of new ones. The formative role was even more useful than the reactive role, as it became possible to vet ideas before working them into concrete proposals. In some cases, the quality control led to much stronger proposals; in others, it led to a mercy killing for an idea that really wasn't ready for prime time.

Running Meetings Effectively

Division and department meetings are different but equally important communication channels. Although a great deal of administrative work occurs in meetings, most administrators are never trained in how to structure and run meetings. Consequently, many meetings are simply awful: ill-focused, overly long, unproductive, and easily hijacked by blowhards' well-rehearsed rants.

For small-group working meetings, it's usually best to have a short agenda and a limited time frame. The chair should not orate, but should be conscientious in the role of traffic cop, making sure that nobody hogs too much airtime or goes too far afield. Academics are good at going beyond the topic at hand and grounding a present issue in much larger questions; the challenge for the chair is to keep people focused on what can actually be done.

For larger meetings, such as academic division meetings, it's usually best to have a longer agenda and a more assertive chair role. I had the best luck with a list of about ten items, the first several of which were strictly informational and, whenever possible, positive. ("Congratulations to Prof. Patterson, who successfully defended her dissertation last month. I'm sorry, I mean congratulations to Dr. Patterson!") Quickly knocking down a few agenda items gives a feeling of progress and also establishes that the chair has the meeting well in hand. Setting a relatively quick pace establishes an expectation and helps convey the idea that long-winded speeches would be out of place.

Of course, there are times when the larger philosophical discussions have to take place. But those occasions should be clearly identified as such, and when they happen, they should be restricted to a single topic. And even there, the ultimate goal is not discussion for its own sake—an occupational hazard of academia—but proposals that can be enacted. Whatever the agenda item is, it should have some sort of logical conclusion to it. That could be applause for the professor who defended her dissertation, or the formation of a committee to work on a self-study, but it should lead somewhere.

I had great luck, too, with establishing a running agenda item noted as "follow-up on issues from last meeting." Frequently, faculty would ask questions during division meetings that I couldn't answer immediately. I'd answer with "Let me get back to you," which initially led to some grumbling. But when the following meeting featured public answers to those questions, acknowledging the people who asked, it became clear that "Let me get back to you" wasn't just a polite dismissal; it was an actual promise. As the promises were kept, they gained credibility, and the quality of discussion improved palpably.

Running good meetings is not magic. Deans neglect the techniques of leading good meetings at their own (and everybody else's!) peril.

Weighing In on Academic Issues

At the level of the two-year college, academic and curricular decisions are based on several factors, each of which can conflict with the others at various times.

Credit Transfers

One issue is transferability. Four-year residential colleges with minimal transfer populations are free to experiment with interdisciplinary freshman seminars, January sessions, noncredit graduation requirements (like swim tests), and the like. Community colleges with significant transfer populations generally can't do those things.

In most cases, there's no blanket guarantee that courses will transfer from one college to another, even when they're accredited by the same agency; sometimes, state colleges won't take certain credits from community colleges in their own state (which raises the ethical question of having the taxpayers subsidize the same class twice).

Typically, students who transfer have to declare an intended major at the destination college. When they do that, the destination college usually allows the department of the intended major to decide which credits to accept and which not to. In most cases, the destination department has no issue with the courses outside the major, but will frequently become unreasonably picky about courses within the major. In candid conversations, the phrase that usually comes up is the unwillingness to "give away too many credits." The problem here is that there's a fundamental conflict of interest in asking people whose jobs depend on credit hours taught to decide how many credit hours to accept in transfer.

Courses outside the major generally receive less scrutiny, as long as they fit in certain predetermined slots. I've never seen a college balk at accepting credits for Composition 1 and 2, for example. Those are industry-standard courses, required at most places, and everyone knows how to account for them. For an art major, say, I'd fully expect Intro to Psych and almost any college-level math course to transfer without incident, but I wouldn't be surprised to see a program balk at some of the 200-level (sophomore) art classes.

Private colleges are free to do whatever they wish with transfer credits. Public colleges and universities have to answer to the state, though, so there's usually some sort of "general education block" that the state expects the destination college to accept in total. Those blocks are typically checklists— nine credits of humanities, six credits of social science, and the like.

The checklists are intended to smooth the transfer process, and to some extent they do. They codify expectations, and transfer counselors at most community colleges keep those lists at the ready to help them advise students in constructing schedules that will maximize their transferability. But the checklists become de facto restrictions on what the two-year colleges can teach. Does the three-credit interdisciplinary freshman seminar fall under humanities, social science, or science? Does the noncredit graduation requirement transfer? I've seen some educationally valid initiatives fall victim to the tyranny of the checklist.

There's also the inconvenient fact that what one college calls a 200-level course, another one will call a 300-level. In the social sciences, it's not unusual for a four-year college to give its statistical methods course a 200-level designation, but then refuse to accept stats classes in transfer. When you get into the more specialized courses within a given major, there's typically no governing authority that dictates which electives fall into the sophomore year (and therefore well within bounds for a community college) and which fall into the junior year. The distinction is somewhat arbitrary, so it's often made based on economic or personnel considerations rather than educational ones.

Remedial (or developmental) courses don't transfer, but they're required of most students. Their ineligibility for transfer is often a source of student complaints ("I don't want to take anything that doesn't count . . ."), but it also allows for more freedom for the college to experiment. I'm locked into a certain number of credit hours for freshman composition, but I'm not locked into anything for developmental English; that means I can theoretically try multiple different approaches to developmental English and see which works best. (Of course, other constraints frequently limit that freedom: financial aid assumes a credit-hour system, for example, and faculty union contracts often do, too.)

Although the public doesn't often recognize it, community colleges don't just send students out on transfer; they also receive them. We get lateral transfers from other community colleges, and we get "reverse transfers" from four-year colleges.

Lateral transfers are usually driven by changes in students' personal lives. Somebody did a semester or two at her local community college after graduating high school, dropped out for a job, and bounced around for a while. Now it's a few years later, she's moved for a job, and she's coming back to school.

Reverse transfers are more sensitive. In my observation, they're usually pretty immediate; it's less common to get reverse transfers with five-year-old credits (though it does happen). A surprising percentage of our new spring enrollments are reverse transfers who went away to four-year schools in the fall and either flunked out or left for other reasons (most commonly either financial or familial). I've heard parents complain with astonishing frankness that their kid drank his way through a $20,000 semester at a private college and that they've sent the kid to the community college as a sort of punishment. I have to admit to being a little insulted every time I hear it, but the truth is that some students just can't resist the temptations of dorm life at eighteen and need a little more focus. I've also heard parents say that Junior has no idea what he wants to study, so they'd rather have Junior figure it out at community college tuition levels and living at home than at $50,000 a year in a dorm. There's something to that.

With reverse transfers, of course, the community college has to decide what to do with, for example, that interdisciplinary seminar. In my observation, community colleges tend to be less territorial about that sort of thing than the four-year schools, probably because at this level we simply accept transfer as a fact of life.

Some states have recently started paying attention to the retroactive reverse transfer, by which a student who transferred from a community college to a four-year school prior to finishing the two-year degree transfers some credits back to pick up the associate's. In part, proposals to facilitate this kind of reverse transfer are attempts to work around a flaw in the way that graduation rates are calculated. In the current system, a student who does, say, one year at a community college and then transfers to a four-year school counts as a dropout for the community college, even if she actually finishes the four-year degree on time. Supporters of community colleges have long argued—correctly—that this artificially dampens the graduation rates by which community colleges are judged.

If more students who transferred early participated in this kind of reverse transfer, community college graduation rates would improve. But it's not clear to me why the student would bother. For a student who drops out in the junior year, an associate's degree is a good consolation prize, but for a student who is well on her way, I'm not sure I see the appeal.

In the private-college sector, the issues are different. Over the past several years, as the economics of the nonelite private colleges have become more tenuous, I've seen private colleges become more receptive to transfer students. Tuition-driven colleges that struggle with attrition are starting to figure out that a student who was able to complete an associate's degree is a low risk for two more years, as that student has already proven the ability to get her stuff together sufficiently to complete a program successfully. The elite schools haven't faced this pressure, and the four-year public schools are still largely swamped with applicants, but those more tenuous private colleges are figuring out that new community college grads are the next great demographic to tap.

The new openness has manifested itself in "articulation agreements" of unprecedented generosity. Although every college has some variation on a residency requirement, or a minimum number of credits that have to be taken at that college before the degree will bear that college's name, I've seen some private colleges offer to take an unusually high number of transfer credits just to get students in the door. This approach basically functions as a loss leader: allow more transfer credits per student, but make it up with more students. It's a great deal for students, who get a private college degree at a remarkable discount; it's a great deal for the community college, which gets to teach credits that often go well into the third year; and it's a great deal for the destination college, which sees its enrollment numbers boom with very low risk students. I expect to see this trend accelerate in the next several years.

Curricular Drift: Losing the Plot and Losing Students

True story: a department chair at my college crusaded for years to make English 101 a prerequisite for the intro course to his discipline. The course necessarily involved sophisticated reading and writing, he argued, and it was insulting and absurd to suggest that students who couldn't perform both of those tasks at the college level could succeed in the class.

After years of struggle, he won. He got the prerequisite. What happened?

Enrollments in the intro course dropped precipitously. The same chair who had spent years decrying low standards for the students in the class abruptly started decrying low enrollments. Shockingly, gatekeeping keeps people out. Who knew?

Several different departments repeated that dance over the years, until the college reached a point at which students who hadn't placed out of, or completed, their developmental coursework had relatively few options for filling out their schedules. (Many students needed full-time status for financial aid reasons, which meant that they had to carry at least twelve credits at a time.) Only a few scattered courses were available to them. So they flooded those courses, and everything else suffered.

It was easy for the college to fall into this trap—and it certainly wasn't the first to do so—because most curriculum committees work on one proposal at a time. Their job is to review proposals as they come in. If, say, the Psychology Department wants to add a prerequisite to its intro course, the fact that Sociology already did isn't taken as a strike against it; if anything, Sociology's move is taken as precedent.

Every individual change along those lines usually makes sense on its own terms. If you're considering only the proposal before you, and not the larger context, it makes perfect sense to vote for it. But the one-proposal-at-a-time model can easily lead to unintended consequences for students, as prerequisites multiply to the point that a college unconsciously creates curricular currents into which many students fall by default.

Curricular questions are dangerous ground for deans. On one level, deans are directly responsible for ensuring the academic quality of the offerings at a college, and are typically called on to troubleshoot when students run into odd curricular dead ends. Deans are also responsible for instructional staffing, whether directly or indirectly, and staffing needs are directly related to the shape of the curriculum. Get a course required, and your department suddenly has a claim on more resources; get a requirement dropped, and your department goes to the end of the line. Anyone who assumes that departments don't quickly gauge the economic impact of curriculum proposals has never watched a discussion of changes to general education requirements. The discussion moves from idealistic invocations of the well-rounded student to straight-up horse-trading, and back again, with dizzying speed.[2]

That said, though, the bargain that most faculty hold in their heads is that the administration controls the budget, but the faculty controls the curriculum. Curriculum is dangerous ground for administrators, and should be trod lightly, when trod at all.

The best solution I've found to the dilemmas around curriculum has been for administrators to use the bully pulpit to ask questions, but to leave the answers to the faculty. If you show, over time, that you can be trusted to uphold your end of the bargain, you may find that you earn some credibility when it comes to setting the agenda. Asking whether it makes sense to channel thousands of developmental students into the same three electives will probably do more good than challenging each new proposal as it comes up. If you can restrict yourself to the level of asking questions and encouraging rational structures, rather than mucking around in the horse-trading, you'll do better by both yourself and the college over time.

Student Retention

"Retention" refers to students coming back for subsequent semesters. Ideally, a student enrolls full-time, sticks around for the prescribed length of the program, and graduates to a good job. That's the best case, and it actually happens for a small fraction of students. That's true in both the for-profit and community college worlds. At the for-profit college where I began my administrative career, there was a low-level culture war between those who saw FPU as a college that happened to make money, and those who saw it as a business that happened to sell education. On the ground, the usual tension was the relationship between academic standards and student retention. The same issues play out at community colleges—with some important differences.

At FPU, students dropped out at a relatively high rate. Sometimes they just "stopped out" for a semester and came back; that was tricky to coordinate within a cohort scheduling model, but it wasn't the end of the world. The real concern was the student who just dropped out and walked away.

As the upper management at FPU never tired of reminding us, it cost much more to recruit a new student than it did to bring back a continuing one.[3] Accordingly, for all the effort FPU put into marketing and admissions, it also put real and sustained pressure on the academic side to keep students coming back for more. After all, in business terms, a retained student is a repeat customer.

The obvious danger in that system is that giving failing grades can look, to the business office, like driving customers away. (It was true that lower GPAs tended to correlate with lower retention rates.) On the flip side, many faculty were concerned that being too promiscuous with grades would lead to graduating incompetent students, which in turn would devalue the degree with prospective employers and gradually eviscerate the college's reason for being.

When enrollments were booming, the conflict was generally pretty mild. When classes are full to capacity and there's a line out the door for more, a little attrition isn't necessarily a bad thing. And as long as the profits were strong, the business folks were willing to let the academics have a little latitude. It wasn't worth the fight.

But when enrollments cratered and every student was suddenly crucial, the pressure on faculty to pass (almost) everybody increased dramatically. At that point, the conflict became much more blunt, and students' sense of entitlement rose accordingly. It didn't take long for students to figure out that they were in the driver's seat, and it quickly became commonplace for students to complain to deans about homework. (I vividly recall a student complaining to me that she had told her professor that she was a working adult, yet he assigned homework *anyway*! I shrugged and mentioned something about college being like that.)

In community colleges, the weight tends to slide to the other end of the fulcrum. Many faculty were themselves very good students, often in severely competitive environments, and at some level they've carried that perspective with them. (I confess that I did, too, in my first years of teaching.) The old "Look to your left, look to your right; one of you will pass" model—"weeding them out," as it's often called—is seductive to faculty, as it places the entire burden of failure on the student. I'm the expert, says this model, and either you have what it takes or you don't. I'll present the material, you'll get it or not, and the cream will rise to the top. Easy.

The problem with this model, of course, is that it builds high levels of failure into the system. It tends to recreate the social-economic inequalities of the outside world and to bless them with a patina of personal merit. If you follow this model all the way out, it's hard to avoid the conclusion that rich white kids are simply better people than poor kids of color. Just look at all their merit!

For those of us who believe that good teaching actually matters, though, high levels of failure suggest some falling down on both sides. The high-minded view of retention looks at high dropout rates as a sign of system failure, rather than individual failure, as the point of the system is to serve individuals. Yes, there will always be some students who are simply beyond help at any given moment—too hostile, too stoned, too distracted, whatever—but to assume that the level we have now is as good as it could ever get is selling some good people short.

Moreover, from a taxpayer's perspective, it's clear that community colleges aren't just there to serve the elite. The elite already have plenty of colleges of their own. If community colleges simply reinforce the negative messages that many students picked up in the K–12 system—you're dumb, you can't learn, other people are better than you—then it's hard to justify their continued existence. There's enough unsubsidized arrogance in the world that we don't need to subsidize more.

The high-minded view of retention says that plenty more students have the ability to succeed than currently do, and that some meaningful proportion of that missed potential can be unlocked by reengineering colleges to meet actual student needs. The right set of improvements doesn't involve excessive hand-holding, and it certainly doesn't involve lowering standards. It means ensuring that students have academic advisers who know what they're talking about and who take the time to actually engage with them; providing free tutoring services for high-risk classes, so that students who are willing to put in the time to improve will have the opportunity; taking textbook costs seriously, so that students whose finances are tight don't try to skate through a semester without the books. (I've seen it done.)

On a broader level, it can also mean things like "intrusive advisement," or mandatory new student orientations, or strong support for a broad array of student clubs and organizations, or making sure there's enough legal parking that students can actually get to class and not pay a second tuition in the form of tickets or towing fees.

However, from the perspective of a professor who isn't involved in much, if any, of these kinds of efforts, calls for "student success" can sound suspiciously close to "go easy on them." For people who paid their dues in the dog-eat-dog system when they rose through the ranks, this feels like selling out. And there's enough financial incentive for tuition-driven colleges (either for-profit or nonprofit) to try to keep "customers" happy that there's some prima facie plausibility to taking the "selling out" thesis literally.

Worse, some colleges actually embrace the darker side of retention and thereby justify the cynical interpretation. Because it takes far more money to attract a new customer than to keep an existing one, a college with a tight bottom-line focus could easily fall into the trap of essentially telling its faculty that the customer is always right.

The arguments against watering down grades should be obvious, but some people still don't get it.

First, there's the moral argument. Lowering standards just to lower standards offends most people's sense of right and wrong.

Second is the "purpose" argument. Education isn't supposed to be just a fancy way to serve time outside the labor force; it's supposed to help students acquire capacities and information they wouldn't have acquired otherwise. Making students work for it is a time-tested way to get them to do their part.

Third is the "reputation" argument. If employers or destination colleges start to notice that the graduates of a particular college just don't cut it relative to others, they'll wind down their recruiting there. Once a college gets tagged as a diploma mill, its ability to recruit new students suffers badly. Which leads to the fourth argument.

Often, a short-term good does long-term harm. Yes, lowering the standards right now will probably have a quick payoff next semester. But over time, being known as an academic joke will make it harder to sustain the continued existence of the college. Donors don't like to contribute to places that aren't respected. The better students will start to steer clear, and a lowering of standards that started out as voluntary could quickly become self-reinforcing. It's notable that the colleges known for very high academic standards—Yale, Swarthmore, Williams—have excellent retention.

A college that intends to stick around for more than a year or two is well advised to clarify with its faculty what it means when it says "retention." I've never heard a professor argue against, say, the existence of a tutoring center. Someone may have at some point, but I've never heard it. A well-designed program of support for students with disabilities will help with retention by helping students reach a high bar rather than by lowering the bar for them; that way, when the students graduate, they do so without apology or asterisk.

Administrators have to walk a difficult line here. It's certainly true that you want to protect students against professors who are either arbitrarily difficult or who are so incompetent that students' low grades wind up as accurate reflections of how little they learned. (Common final exams across multiple sections are great for that. If you run thirty sections of College Algebra, and Professor Jones's two sections come in two standard deviations below the mean, it's fair to ask some questions of and about Professor Jones.) Basic fairness suggests that a student shouldn't get a substantially lower grade for the same work simply by luck of the draw.

At the same time, though, pay too much attention to pass rates, and faculty will get the message—whether you mean it or not—that they're safer if they're easy.

Dealing with Helicopter Parents

In the age of helicopter parents—that is, "concerned" parents who won't stop hovering around their children—most administrators can expect to deal with angry parents from time to time.

Rules come in particularly handy in these situations. The first one to learn is FERPA. The Family Educational Rights and Privacy Act sets some relatively strict guidelines as to which personal information about students you can share, and with whom, in the absence of a signed waiver. FERPA is your friend. And that isn't just evasiveness, either; you don't usually know the backstory behind a request for information, and sometimes, giving information to the wrong person can lead to real harm. For example, letting an abusive boyfriend know his girlfriend's class schedule can put the girlfriend in harm's way.

Explaining FERPA also gives you an opening, if you need one, to explain to the parent the differences between high school and college. Given the real issues in many public K–12 districts, some parents have learned to be hands-on advocates for their kids, and some of them have trouble unlearning that when the kid gets to college.

Some parents also believe that the act of writing the tuition check entitles them to access to whatever they want to know and to whomever they want to see. Alas, no.

FERPA is not absolute. Aside from voluntary written waivers by students, there are also exceptions for emergencies having to do with physical safety. If a professor or staff member has reason to believe that a student is in such a state as to be a real danger to himself or others, she can report that without fear of liability. In the wake of the Virginia Tech massacre, many colleges stepped back from dogmatic readings of FERPA and established their own internal protocols for threat assessment.

Still, exceptions aside, the basic idea behind FERPA is that students are adults and are responsible for their own affairs. If a kid cheats on a test, gets caught, and fails the class, I say the kid just learned a valuable life lesson. If a kid takes too many classes at once and discovers his own limits, that too is worth knowing. Learning how to struggle, and even learning how to fail and get back up again, is crucial, and it won't happen if Mommy and Daddy are always bailing you out.

Coping with "Academic Freedom"

As a rhetorical device, "academic freedom" is a baseball bat with which some faculty will beat to a pulp anything they don't like. That's unfortunate, not least because academic freedom properly understood is so crucial to the enterprise.

I have seen academic freedom used as an excuse to not show up to class, to not hold office hours, to viciously attack administrators personally in public, to commingle student organization funds with personal funds, and to ignore both course descriptions and departmentally chosen textbooks. It properly covers none of these.

Academic freedom inheres in the college as an institution, not in the individual professor. This means that it is up to the college as a whole to determine what shall be taught and by whom. In practice, this means that if someone is hired to teach, say, digital circuitry, and instead spends most of the class time discussing civil war reenactments, he is not protected by the cloak of academic freedom. He is properly subject to discipline, up to and including termination.

Academic freedom was intended to protect the pursuit of truth in both the classroom and in scholarly research. Partisans of tenure like to argue that only tenure can protect the pursuit of uncomfortable truths. (I believe that contractual language can accomplish the same thing; but that's another book.) I disagree with the connection to tenure, but agree that the pursuit of truth in the classroom and in scholarly research is crucial. A course on, say, modern political thought has to be able to address communism, or it simply will not achieve its purpose, just as a course on human biology needs to be able to address evolution. An economist in a tobacco-producing state should not be subject to sanction for noting the economic irrationality of tobacco subsidies, nor should a historian of the civil rights movement be sanctioned for noting the documented human frailties of some of its leaders.

But the partisans of tenure often take academic freedom much further than that. They move from their areas of substantive expertise to the governance of the college as a whole. The ultimate expression of this conception of academic freedom is the vote of no confidence.

Although votes of no confidence are a timeworn tactic in American higher education, they come divorced from the institutional setting in which they make sense. They come originally from parliamentary government.

In a parliamentary system, the chief executive (typically called the prime minister) is elected by parliament itself, rather than by the voters. The idea is that the majority party in parliament should be able to appoint the chief executive so that it can enact its platform; "divided government" such as we routinely have in the United States, in which one party controls Congress while another controls the presidency, is nearly impossible in a parliamentary system. (The exception occurs when a cluster of small parties governs by coalition, but coalitions are inherently unstable and tend to be short lived.)

A vote of no confidence occurs when enough members of the majority party have lost faith in the leadership that they side with the minority party, and vote to force a new election. They have the right to do so because the prime minister reports to them.

Transplanted to higher education in the United States, votes of no confidence are entirely symbolic. The faculty is not a parliament, and the president or chancellor is not a prime minister. The president or chancellor is selected by the board of trustees, not by the faculty. A savvy board will take the faculty voice into consideration, but ultimately, the vote of the board is dispositive.

In a literal sense, then, faculty votes of no confidence have no standing. Choosing the president is not a faculty role; therefore, efforts to do so are not properly protected by academic freedom.

That said, though, it would be unwise to simply dismiss votes of no confidence as the overreaching that they literally are. They are more fruitfully understood as expressions of frustration, even if they aren't phrased that way. Even when the efforts seem misbegotten in themselves, it is usually well worthwhile to try to understand, if not address, the causes of the frustration underlying the vote.

Finding Balance

Work-life balance is an issue when you're recruiting and retaining faculty, but it's an issue for administrators, too. Administrators have to find that balance to survive in the job, and I expect that this will become ever more critical as the next generation makes its way through the pipeline.

Deans and other academic administrators may think of themselves as managers, and in most ways, they are. But they are also ceremonial figures, with ceremonial duties. In my own case, I find that the stretch from mid-April to graduation is almost comically overstuffed with evening events: end-of-year celebrations, performances, galas, thank-you dinners, and the like. Every single one of these events is worthy and fine in its own way, but the accumulation of them can be backbreaking. That's especially true if, like me, you have kids at home.

At many colleges, the ranks of deans and above are still filled by people from the boomer cohort, most of whom either have grown children or don't have children at all. But as that cohort slowly makes its way toward retirement, the generation behind it—my own—will have to step up. And in this cohort, for most of us, the expectations on mothers are as high as ever, and on fathers are higher than they have ever been.[4]

As is true for the workforce at large, this can play out in different ways. One way is to just keep working everybody harder and to replace burnouts as needed. That's the default path, the path of least resistance; and it's easy to fall into unthinkingly. It's also pathological. Among other flaws, it effectively restricts the leadership ranks to people who aren't dealing with many of the daily life issues faced by the rest of the workforce. When that happens, the blind spots don't change, and the pattern continues.

Alternately, and more optimistically, colleges could adjust the expectations to gradually become more sustainable. In some ways, this is already happening; it's much less common than it once was, for example, for entire departments to go out drinking together after work. The premium on extracurricular face time for faculty has faded, and most of us see that change as positive.

But for the leadership, it's still there, and quite strong. Invitations are spurned at a cost. That's especially true if you have the bad luck to succeed someone who attended everything; suddenly your nonattendance at some event is a Statement.

I saw this directly in my own career. I stepped into an environment in which deans were expected to show up to nearly everything, and they did. I tried to keep up, but after a while, the demands on home life became intolerable. Any evening I wasn't home, the child-care duties fell entirely to my wife. When that happened three evenings a week for a month or more, the imbalance in child care ran headfirst into our generational expectation of shared parenting.

In the short term, the other deans and I handled it by establishing an informal rotation. When an event crossed the academic divisions, we'd take turns attending it. That way, we were able to maintain some sort of visible ceremonial presence without burning ourselves out.

Between the cost pressures that will likely start to shrink the administrative ranks—that already started happening in the Great Recession of 2009—and the shift in generational attitudes, I expect that the ceremonial part of the dean's role will shrink in the future. In some ways, that's likely to be a good thing. I'd like to see more parents among the ranks of deans, as they'll have a visceral understanding of some of the struggles of young faculty. It would also open up the positions to a larger range of applicants, which portends, all else being equal, a higher level of talent in the role. Unfortunately, the ceremonial obligations will probably be replaced, at least to some degree, by a greater expectation for fundraising.

Acting Like a Dean

Presidents are largely concerned with external relations, and vice presidents are often consumed with policy and budgets. Faculty are consumed with teaching and all that goes along with it. Deans have the challenge of providing a steady, consistent presence that can remind the upper administration of the concerns of the faculty and can translate the concerns of upper administration to the faculty. Deans are the folks who put out fires with student issues, work closely with struggling faculty, and hold together an organization whose logic is built on not holding together very well. It's not an easy job.

Deans also need to manage themselves emotionally. People follow cues from authority figures, even when those cues are unintentional. If a dean is evasive, or panicky, faculty and staff will respond accordingly. A dean who projects calm confidence, in contrast, stands a better chance of bringing out the best in the people around her. If the faculty know that someone reliable is minding the store, they're better able to focus on their own work. And just as the townsfolk eventually disbelieved the boy who cried "wolf," a manager who projects an air of crisis all the time won't have credibility when a real crisis happens. If you gain a reputation for being level-headed, then your rare cries of "wolf" will actually bring attention.

The hardest part of that emotional control, in my experience, is in avoiding the temptation to hit back when you get attacked. I learned early, and by accident, that hierarchy is an amplifier; a comment that seemed witty coming from a professor just seemed mean coming from a dean. This is where "transparency" hits its limits; no matter how true they may seem in the moment, many comments are best left unsaid.

The best approach I've found for that is thinking in terms of consequences, rather than accuracy. Yes, Professor Anderson may be a pompous jackass, but would saying so actually help? It's better over the long term to maintain a confident professionalism and to let Professor Anderson suffer by the contrast. In the meantime, you'll avoid the collateral damage that would have occurred when other people saw only the frustrated response, rather than the provocations, and decided that you're vindictive or capricious. Play the long game, and trust that over time, the petty stuff will come out in the wash.

As frustrating as the role can sometimes be, though, good deans provide a constancy and a predictability that allow the creative professionals—that is, the faculty—to do their best work. By setting a climate around transparent policies, clear and consistent rules, impersonal fairness, and real listening, a good dean can prevent the entropic tendencies of faculty culture from ripping the college apart. It's as much art as science, and it's easy to miss if you aren't looking closely; like good film editing, when it's done well, things just sort of work. But when it's done badly, the damage is real.

SAVING COMMUNITY COLLEGES

A FEW MODEST PROPOSALS

SO FAR, I'VE SKETCHED A PRETTY GLOOMY PICTURE. Higher education in general, as we know it, is at a crossroads. Its midcentury goal of what Benjamin Barber (1992) called "an aristocracy of everyone" has become unsustainable. The next generation of leaders won't have the option of coasting and waiting for the money to come back; it will have to make some choices.

If it follows the default path, higher education will simply mirror the growing economic bifurcation in America as a whole: the elites will get more elite, the low-end providers will have more low-end clientele, and the (nonprofit) middle will fade, pulled either up or down. This will create a major opening in between for for-profit and other alternative providers.

That bifurcation poses a real challenge for the public sector. Historically, public higher education has generally been associated with the middle class. Consequently, as the middle class dissolves and becomes absorbed by the two extremes, public education may find itself in a difficult position. As we have seen over the past few decades, institutions that are identified in the public mind with poor people have been first stigmatized and then, over time, defunded. Eventually, if the past is any guide, this bodes ill for the survival of community colleges as institutions of higher education; at best, they may be remade into (or relegated to the status of) adult literacy centers.

Alternately, the next generation of leaders could decide to stop being buffeted by external forces, and start remaking community colleges in ways that both play to their historic strengths and bode well for their long-term survival and even prosperity. But doing that will require political will—no small thing in the short term—and a well-considered strategy that takes no existing dogma as sacred.

Certainly, one of the most dramatic developments in American higher education over the past twenty years or so has been the rise of the for-profits. Even in the face of their rapid growth, most of traditional higher ed either ignores them or simply assumes that they're irrelevant. I consider that an egregious mistake. They emerged for a reason, and they succeed for a reason. Although I agree that it would be absurd to simply copy them blindly, I suggest that they offer lessons from which we can benefit.

In later sections of this chapter, I'll outline some of the changes that, if adopted quickly, could help right the ship. But first, let's take a look at for-profit colleges and the lessons they might offer for higher education in general and community colleges in particular.

Inside For-Profits

The fastest-growing sector of higher education in America is the for-profits. This has been true for several decades, but the dominant non-profit sector is only just beginning to notice. And much of the notice it has taken has been alarmist or dismissive, based on caricature rather than serious analysis. To the extent that many in traditional higher ed have noticed the for-profits, they've drawn the wrong lessons from them, such as these: advertise to death, specialize in the hot field of the day, crack down on tough grading, slavishly follow employer dictates on curriculum, pay admissions reps on commission, de-emphasize traditional academic subjects, de-skill individual faculty in the name of standardization, and blur the line between financial aid and sales.

To the extent that these are the lessons drawn, then folks in traditional higher ed are entirely right to regard the for-profits with suspicion, if not outright hostility.[1] But the for-profits do some things well, and there's no reason not to learn from them.

As mentioned earlier, I worked at a major for-profit—you've heard of it—from 1997 to 2003. I started as an adjunct, then was hired after a semester to the full-time faculty. I taught full-time for a little over three years before moving into administration. By the time I left, my ranks there had included

- Adjunct
- Full-time professor

- Department chair
- Associate dean
- Dean

What made that path possible, of course, was rapid growth. Unlike the rest of higher education at that time, the organization was expanding rapidly, opening new branches all over the country at the rate of several per year. New campuses were staffed at the leadership level, initially, with transfers from existing campuses, which created considerable updraft. By being in the right place at the right time and not turning up my nose at the prospect of "crossing over to the dark side," I was able to move up quickly.

It wasn't until I moved to my first community college deanship that I fully appreciated just how unusual that ascent actually was.

When I left FPU, I held the rank of dean and was thirty-four years old. At FPU, I didn't stand out by virtue of age. When I arrived at the community college as a dean, my age was two standard deviations below the mean for the full-time faculty there. Department chairs in my area openly referred to me as "kiddo." In several departments, the younger cohort was in its fifties and had been there for "only" twenty-five or thirty years. It would be fair to describe my reception as cool.

Yet when I got the local history and did the math, I realized that many of the Former Administrators Returned to Teaching—FARTs—were themselves younger than I was when they started. It had just been so long ago that they had forgotten. An entire generation had aged in place together, with all that that implies.

I couldn't shake the sense of having traveled back in time. The community college was far more bureaucratic and gossipy than FPU, with an inwardly focused status obsession that I couldn't make myself take seriously. But it was actually far more representative of the status quo of most of American higher education than FPU was, at least for now.

Attracting Fresh Blood

When I worked at FPU, one of the bigwigs from the home office came to campus about once per year to give a pep talk. At some point in each pep talk, he'd refer to FPU's "secret weapon: private investment capital." I didn't really appreciate it at the time, but he was right.

The advantage of the proprietary sector is that it experiences growth as profitable. Because students pay more than the full cost of their education, more students bring with them more profit. Growth more than pays for itself. And when the college is publicly traded as a stock, the start-up costs for new campuses can be covered readily through the capital raised from investors who see the growth and profitability and want in.

When I arrived at FPU in the late 1990s, it had been growing at a rapid clip for some time. This meant that it was hiring. Given the choice between adjuncting at a traditional college and holding down a real job with a real salary at a proprietary, I made the rational choice.

In the higher ed blogosphere, there's a default assumption that for-profits are exploitative, and nonprofits virtuous. From the perspective of a new PhD in the late 1990s who needed a job, though, the reverse was true. The nonprofit sector was more than happy to work me endlessly at piece rates, but had no intention of hiring me to a living wage. The for-profit sector, in contrast, presented opportunity.

The divergence of opportunities has significant ramifications for nonprofit institutions. Back when new PhD's could find desirable jobs in the traditional sector, there was no reason to fear that for-profits could even start to compete on the same turf. They might do fine with cosmetology or auto repair, but the idea that they might, say, confer accredited "business" degrees was just otherworldly. Where would they get the faculty?

Now, of course, decades of overproduction of PhD's has led to an ample pool of job candidates. In their zeal to justify their own graduate programs, the major research universities have given the for-profits an opening to hire terrific young faculty on the cheap. In my time at FPU, because it was expanding rapidly and nobody else was, it was able to gather a large and vibrant group of youngish PhD's who were excited just to have full-time teaching jobs. Most of us were a little irked at having landed there, but it beat adjuncting.

Now that just about any educational start-up can hire a strong cadre of faculty without even trying, one significant barrier to entry is down. Although there are variables across fields and geography—it's easier to find prospective English professors in New York City than it is to find prospective nursing professors in Terre Haute, say—the basic idea still holds. The nonprofits have sown the seeds of their own destruction in the form of their own graduate students.

Filling a Niche

Of course, that doesn't mean that all is well and good in the land of the for-profits.

Most for-profits don't style themselves as "comprehensive," in the manner of comprehensive public universities. Instead, they pick a few marketable niches and focus on those. "Marketable" in this case is double-edged: it refers both to marketability of graduates as workers and to marketability to prospective students. I've never seen a proprietary with a philosophy major.

The advantages of the "niche" strategy are several. It allows the benefits of specialization, for one. When the entire college offers only four majors, it's easy to staff the four majors pretty thoroughly and become the locally dominant player in those four areas. (For example, FPU was well connected with local employers in its own fields, as it provided so many graduates in them.) Cohort tracking is relatively easy, because you're dividing the students into just a few groups, rather than the hundred or so that a comparably sized traditional college might. You can also establish a pretty clear brand identity in the marketplace, which is crucial when going after first-generation students. They might not be able to distinguish one state college from the next, but they have a clear idea that FPU means that "you'll get a job." Although traditional faculty often look down on the pecuniary motive among students, it's real, and given the cost of college, it's rational.

Of course, if you replace the term "comprehensive" with "diversified," you can see the hazard of the niche strategy. If you put most of your eggs in one basket and that basket suddenly goes out of fashion, you're in trouble. I saw that happen at FPU in the early 2000s when the tech bubble burst, and the whole computer networking field imploded. When nearly half of the students majored in one field and that one field suddenly turned cold, things got ugly fast. Within less than a year, discussion on campus shifted from expansion to layoffs, and one of my first tasks as a dean was to decide whom to fire. Introductions to administration don't get much nastier than that.

Serving the "Customer"

One of the for-profits' strengths is a strong focus on helping students navigate the federal financial aid paperwork. Anyone who has done battle with a FAFSA (Free Application for Federal Student Aid) form knows that the hoops you have to jump through are many and varied; for a first-generation college student with a shaky academic background, the process can be utterly opaque. The "concierge" model of helping students through—what in nonprofits is usually called a "resource specialist" and only found in grant-funded programs—is normal there, and effective.

They also tend to have very well staffed and internally valued career services offices. When I was at FPU, a course called Career Development was actually a graduation requirement in every program. Students did everything from personality assessments to resume writing to rehearsals for job interviews. The course was designed on the assumption that the cultural capital to interview well for professional positions is largely the province of the upper middle class, so helping the working-class students compete required deliberate attention to what the kids at Swarthmore could largely take for granted. The subject matter came closer to the old "finishing school" idea than to a traditional academic subject, but it was useful and badly needed.

In the community college world, this requirement would be radioactive, and that's a real loss. It's radioactive because it raises the specters of elitism, racism, classism, and all the other objectionable, exclusionary isms that open-door institutions explicitly reject. In the name of diversity, there's a real reluctance to address or even acknowledge the existence of yawning gaps between professional culture and the culture of many of the students. And the culture of traditional higher ed largely encourages that oversight, because the traditional culture dates to a time when higher ed was limited to the children of the elite, who already had cultural capital. To the extent that they didn't, frat and dorm life or sports would take care of it.

Since then, of course, the constituency for college has expanded dramatically, but the old assumptions are still strong. Denying the problem doesn't make it go away, though. I recall advising one of my students at FPU to lose the "do-rag" before his interview; he looked at me quizzically, not understanding how the do-rag could undermine his self-presentation. At a community college, it's unlikely that anyone would feel safe bringing up the do-rag in the first place.

So, what can we learn from the for-profits?

Rethinking the Calendar

The credit hour, as discussed earlier, is one time-based barrier to improved productivity. The other great time-based barrier for most of higher education is the traditional academic calendar. This is another place where we can take a leaf from the for-profits' book. Because they have a more sophisticated understanding of cost than most traditional colleges do, they have been able to see (and act on) the value of rejecting the traditional academic calendar in favor of a twelve-month calendar. This change allows them to reduce the real cost of a degree without reducing tuition. If you can complete eight semesters in slightly under three years (by taking three four-month semesters per year), you've just reduced the opportunity cost of the degree by over a year's salary. That's nothing to sneeze at. This is especially true when attending classes involves making child-care arrangements, sacrificing time with family, and juggling multiple priorities. Knocking a year off of that makes a meaningful difference in people's lives.

(Instructively, the major issue with time to completion at community colleges is that it typically takes much longer than the normative two years. Despite research showing that temporal discontinuity reduces success rates for students, community colleges have clung tenaciously to the traditional calendar.)

Although many nonprofit colleges run summer sessions, those sessions are largely afterthoughts. At my own, for example, the course offerings are determined largely by the interests of "visiting" students who are home for the summer, rather than those of students continuing from the Spring semester. A more deliberate use of the summer as an integral part of the academic year could make a real difference for students, and could also make better use of the college's physical plant.

Of course, implementing this change the right way would take more than simply duplicating the Fall or Spring. Faculty workloads would need careful consideration, given that, as I saw at FPU, twelve months of teaching year after year is a recipe for burnout. But there's no principled reason that "off" semesters couldn't be staggered. Financial aid rules would take serious adjustments, as well. The Obama administration briefly experimented with "year-round" Pell grants, allowing students to carry balances over into summer terms, but quickly dropped the experiment. Community college leaders need to make the case that continuity is key to student success, especially for low-income and nontraditional students, and that the financial aid rules need to adjust in recognition of that.

Year-round calendars would allow greater flexibility for internships and co-ops, as well. Employers who can handle only a few at a time wouldn't be swamped in the summer and bereft in the fall.

Taking Career Services Seriously

Until recently, career services offices have been afterthoughts at many community colleges. They've been shunted into odd corners and left to attract students on their own. Some campuses have identified the futility of that and have responded by dissolving them altogether.

That's a mistake. The classic version of the career services office may have become unsatisfactory, but students still need all sorts of practical guidance. The for-profits are well aware of that; at FPU, for example, the career services office was a powerful internal constituency on campus, and as I mentioned earlier, students in every program had to take a career development course as a graduation requirement. The requirement came from a practical observation that students needed help and that the entire selling point for FPU in the educational marketplace was employability.

A more imaginative use of career services could have real payoff.

For example, sending career counselors into "Introduction to . . ." classes in career-oriented programs can help students identify opportunities in fields of which they were previously unaware. At my current college, for example, we have an Intro to Health Careers course that all pre-nursing students have to take. The career counselor helps explain the various other career options available in the health care field beyond nursing, addressing everything from physicians' assistants to occupational therapists to epidemiologists. Many students had no idea that those fields existed when they enrolled; they chose nursing because they had heard of it and they knew they could make a living doing it. But upon discovering other choices, many students take them. Epidemiology is a great choice for the student who loves the idea of health care but hates the sight of blood.

This use of career services plays to the strengths of community colleges. It also respects students as thoughtful people who might well take other options, if only they were exposed to them. Better, a consensus is forming in the research that suggests that students who know what they want are likelier to persist than students who don't. That makes intuitive sense; having a goal in mind makes sacrifice seem more worthwhile. Offering career advice to students early in their academic careers can make it easier for them to identify goals; once they do that, they're on their way.

Embracing Specialization

This is a delicate subject, but it needs to be addressed.

Community colleges define themselves largely by "access." They have an open-door admissions policy, and they typically develop course offerings based on perceived local needs and interests. Comprehensiveness of course offerings—offering the widest possible range of both transfer and career programs—has historically been one of the ways that community colleges have attempted to fulfill their goal of providing access.

If community colleges are going to survive, though, I suspect that the comprehensive model will have to go the way of the variety show.

As difficult as it is to achieve excellence in any given program, it's that much harder to achieve it across a hundred or more. In practice, the quality of programs at any given college typically ranges from outstanding to we'd-rather-not-discuss-it. Accreditation doesn't really address the issue, because institutional accreditation is across the board. A few programs have their own specific accrediting bodies—engineering and nursing leap to mind—but most programs just fall under the broad institutional umbrella.

Over time, most colleges fall victim to a sort of horizontal mission creep. (Vertical mission creep would involve offering four-year degrees.) They typically start with a liberal arts transfer degree, as that's cheap to provide and easy to explain, and a few career-oriented programs that fit local needs. Over time, though, new needs come along, and the college starts new programs to address them. Given the way that curricula are approved, it's far easier to start programs than it is to shut them down, so the default direction is expansive.

When funding gets tight, it's politically easier to water everything down—typically by increasing the percentage of courses taught by adjuncts—than it is to isolate a few programs for elimination. Reducing the full-time faculty in, say, automotive repair from three to two happens quietly, with almost nobody outside the automotive program even noticing. Eliminating the automotive program generates student protests, negative press, and sometimes even anger from trustees. It's unsurprising that conflict-averse administrations would rather water down the liquor in every bottle in the cabinet than actually throw some bottles out.

That said, though, if quality is the primary concern, I'd rather do a few things well than many things badly. In the age of outcomes assessment, it's getting harder to deny the negative impact of continuing to water down the quality of existing programs. Although colleges that do it get heat for it, I'd expect to see—frankly, hope to see—colleges shift gears and start to pick winners.

The best way to do that from a systemic perspective would be to have different local colleges specialize in different things. If a statewide system of community colleges decided to allocate programs among colleges based on statewide or regional need, rather than having each one run whatever it wants and compete with the others, it could get more bang for its buck where the programs actually run.

Local specialization within a statewide system should not be confused with centralized control at the state level. Identifying one college as a "technical" community college and a nearby one as a transfer-focused college doesn't imply state-level operational control. If anything, improvement over time will require the freedom to experiment, which is likeliest to flourish when individual colleges are free to try different things. The difficult but necessary balance is between clear definitions of mission, which would have to be coordinated at the state level, and operational autonomy at the local level to discover the best ways to fulfill the various missions.

Historically, geography was a compelling counterargument to local specialization; if the local college didn't offer a particular program, then people in that area didn't have access to the program. In the age of the Internet, though, that's becoming less of an issue.

The approval hoops for new programs at the state level play a role, too. It's much harder to gain approval for a new program than it is to ramp up an existing one. Therefore, a college has a disincentive to actually kill a program it thinks might need to come back in the future. It's easier to hedge bets and just keep the thing on life support. Of course, that involves putting vulnerable students through a program that's just on life support.

In the absence of a compelling reason to pick a fight, it has usually been easier just to let attrition do the dirty work. Why take on tenured faculty and insulted trustees if you don't have to?

The rise of the for-profits, though, is changing the equation. For-profits specialize in vocational programs, and they're unabashed proponents of the do-a-few-things-well approach. They're in a position to do to the comprehensive model what narrowly focused cable channels did to the variety show model. They will pick off the people who want a specific thing.

The savvy move for community colleges would be to reap the benefits of their own specialization. They specialize in the first two years of college, which nearly always include some foundational courses in English, math, history, psychology, and the like. They have decades of practice in teaching those, and the potential for becoming industry leaders in doing them well. After all, who gets more practice?

Better yet, the fields in which the for-profits have typically chosen to specialize tend to be capital intensive and relatively high cost. Running history classes is far cheaper than running dental hygienist classes—the equipment costs are far lower, faculty are easier to find, and you can run larger sections. (You also don't have to deal with clinical placements, program-specific accreditations, and the vagaries of narrow local job markets.) The for-profits have started with high-cost programs because they're easy to explain in advertisements, the payoff for students is obvious, and cash-strapped public colleges have sometimes struggled to compete there.

My advice would be to stop trying. Reap the benefits of specialization. Most community colleges started with liberal arts and general education degrees; there's a surprisingly valid market-based argument for returning to those roots. Let the for-profits handle the really expensive majors; other than a few unique areas of historic strength (like nursing), community colleges may be well advised to focus on the fundamentals. To the extent that the public sector needs to support some high-cost, specialized programs, let them be allocated regionally, so that no one campus has to bear too many of them.

That would require some trimming of the curriculum, some jettisoning of programs (and the people who work in them), and a willingness to double down on the basics. More focus would allow for the benefits of more focus. Let the college spend its time and manpower on the educational core, and leave the training to the for-profits.

If community colleges moved more intentionally in this direction, they could realize both academic and economic improvements. The economic improvements would come from having less-expensive programs constitute a larger portion of the curriculum. The academic improvements would come from being able to bring more resources to bear on the classes they do teach. I'd love to be able to do controlled experiments running different versions of the same course side by side to see what works, but that's hard to do and to track when the staff is barely able to keep pace with all the programs we currently have.

A cleaner focus on the liberal arts core would also insulate community colleges to some degree against economic fluctuations. Demand in this industry or that one will wax and wane, but communication skills, quantitative skills, and the ability to make sense of ambiguity will always be useful. (I once heard that the great gift of historical study is a sense of how things don't happen. That can be remarkably useful.) Watering down the core has been a fundamental miscalculation, and it has left community colleges open to devastating competition. It's time to let go of the idea of being all things to all people; survival in the near future will depend on being the best at something. Why not be the best at the core? (Alternately, if the state really wants high-cost vocational programs, it's invited to step up and pay for them.)

Beyond For-Profits: Doing What We Do, Better

Beyond what for-profits can suggest, what else can community college leaders do to help community colleges adapt and thrive?

Killing the Credit Hour

The standard currency for defining credentials is the credit hour, which is defined in terms of normative seat time. (I say "normative" because we use credit hours for online classes, too, even though the concept of seat time makes little sense there. Typically, the credit hours for any given online class are the same as for the in-class counterpart.)

But there's really no reason that needs to be true.

Students accumulate credits toward degrees, achieving the degree when they've hit the magic number of credits (in the right combination) with the right GPA. That's true whether or not the credits actually add up to something coherent and whether or not the student actually perceived the coherence that we're supposed to assume is there.

The credit-hour system has certain advantages. Probably chief among these is that it allows for transferability of courses between institutions. Given the number of students who attend two or more institutions on their way to a bachelor's degree—including community college transfers—this is no small thing. It also lends itself to cross-institutional comparisons on spending, tuition, and the like. The entire financial aid system is based on credit hours. It's a common denominator that has come to hold more functions than it was ever originally intended to hold.

But externally, credit hours mean nothing. They're entirely arbitrary. What employers actually care about, and what we as citizens should actually care about, is ability.

If we're ever going to escape the productivity trap outlined earlier, we need to move away from time-based measures of learning. I support a learning-based measure of learning instead. Define the competencies a student should be able to demonstrate at the end of a course, and at the end of a course of study, base credentials on successfully demonstrating those.

Interestingly, this is actually how most higher education worked prior to the twentieth century. Many colleges and professional schools didn't even give grades, let alone use credit hours; you studied until you demonstrated that you were ready for practice, at which point you left.

The various regional accrediting agencies have attempted to move in this direction to some degree by pushing a program of outcomes assessment. The idea behind outcomes assessment is to measure results, as opposed to inputs, in the name of spurring improvements where the results are falling short.

Broadly speaking, faculty hate outcomes assessment.

In the current context, there's a perfectly logical reason to hate it: it's an add-on. If you have to run both the time-based and the outcomes-based assessments, you're repeating yourself. Many faculty correctly perceive the current scheme of outcomes assessment as extra labor-intensive work for little or no payoff; the financial and programmatic decisions that really matter are still based on credit hours.

But if we were to take the next step—doing away with the credit hour and instead basing credentials on demonstrated competencies—outcomes assessment would suddenly become a lot more meaningful. It would have teeth.[2]

I don't mean to understate the difficulties involved in moving from the current system to the new one. Interinstitutional transfer, for example, would become much trickier. If different colleges define their desired outcomes differently—which I assume would usually be the case—then a student who successfully demonstrated the competencies stressed at college A might have to start all over again at college B. (That's not to deny that colleges play games with transfer credits in the current system; it's just to concede that the potential for gamesmanship could be even worse in the new one.)

That said, though, it's simply indefensible to make students mark time before getting recognition for what they already know, just to ease a bureaucratic question.

If we move to a demonstrated-competency system, then we stop rewarding colleges for making students jump through hoops, and start rewarding them for teaching well. In other words, for the first time in a hundred years, we'd get the incentives right. Resources go where the incentives say they should go, so I'd expect to see colleges start to focus more deliberately on helping students succeed.

An outcomes-based system also opens up the possibility of doing away with the fundamental conflict of interest in having the people who teach also be the people who assign grades. Grade inflation is the term of art for faculty who decide that it's easier to keep the peace by giving higher-than-deserved grades than it would be to fight the good fight. But moving assessment to an external predefined standard recasts the relationship between teacher and student. It's no longer a basic conflict; now it's you and me against the test (or the project or the deadline or the panel).

This model already exists in some professions. Nursing students have to pass the NCLEX exam, and nursing programs are judged, in part, by the percentage of their students who pass. Aspiring lawyers have to pass the bar exam; law schools can be judged by their pass rates. Moving the standard from the idiosyncratic judgment of one person to an external measure makes it much harder to game the system from inside.

Rethinking Developmental Education

If there's any low-hanging fruit for the next generation of leaders who want to make a meaningful difference, developmental education is it. There is nearly universal agreement at this point that the traditional approach to remediation—a series of progressive semester-based courses—is an expensive failure. The data are certainly there to support the idea that the status quo isn't working, and on many campuses, the departments that carry most of the weight of developmental education—English and math, usually—resent it.

Policymakers and national foundations are paying attention to developmental education success rates, and in some cases are even providing resources to do something about them. The Lumina Foundation, for example, has been active in supporting experiments to improve student success in developmental sequences, and the Carnegie Foundation—through its Mathway and Statway projects—is supporting "embedded" or "just in time" remediation, in which students enroll directly in college-level coursework and get extra help on selected topics on an as-needed basis. The Achieving the Dream project—a data-driven attempt to improve student success rates at community colleges across the country—has identified developmental math as a key barrier for students, and has supported all manner of experimentation to improve results. Even many states are getting in on it, pushing everything from "contextualized" remediation—teaching math in the context of a course in the student's major—to accelerated delivery, self-paced delivery, and modularized courses.

Developmental education carries a terrible stigma with the public at large, for reasons both good and ill. It's expensive, its success rates are low, and by definition, it repeats information already taught—and paid for—at the K–12 level. Research by the Community College Research Center, at Columbia University, has shown clearly that students who start at the lowest levels of developmental education have terribly low graduation rates, which raises the question of the point of it all (Edgecombe, 2011). Complete College America (2011), a foundation-supported initiative to improve student success rates, has found that time is the enemy: simply put, the longer it takes to complete a sequence of courses, the more opportunity for life to get in the way. (Less charitably, developmental education also plays into the economic and racial stereotypes that bedevil programs aimed at helping the poor. Although there's nothing admirable about that, it's a political reality, and we ignore it at our peril.) The findings about life getting in the way are consistent with my own college's recent experiments with a two-week January intersession, in which students take just one class, intensely, for two weeks. Pass rates are about fifteen points higher in intersession than during the regular semesters, and the faculty who've taught it have consistently reported that it was the most satisfying teaching they've done. Speed helps.

With financial aid finite, student loan debt burdens a live topic, and the K–12 system continuing to struggle, developmental education is likely to remain an issue for some time. A new leader who makes a difference in developmental education would be very well received.

The savvy administrator will keep in mind, though, that anything involving curriculum is widely considered the faculty's domain. This means that any sustainable innovation will have to be done with the faculty. Avoid, avoid, avoid the temptation to try to declare a new regime of remediation from on high; that's guaranteed to fail. Even though nearly the entire policy and foundation apparatus of the country agrees that the status quo doesn't work—and it's right—any new approach that hopes to succeed can only succeed with the active support of local faculty.

So, how to do that?

I've had good luck with a combination of agenda setting, resources, and careful observation of boundaries. In brief, I've done the following:

1. Outline the definition of the problem—students not making it through the sequence—and the general findings in the literature.

2. Offer time (in the form of course releases) and money (for travel) for faculty to explore what other colleges are doing and to develop a proposal to run locally.

3. Back off for a while and let the faculty hash it out.

4. Agree to run a pilot of a new, shorter sequence, developed by the faculty. Agree up front on what the criteria for success will be and how they will be measured.

Through this approach, the math department came up with a shorter sequence for students who want to go into the algebra-based sequence needed for STEM majors, and a variation on Statway for prospective non-STEM majors. (STEM is the accepted acronym for science, technology, engineering, and math.) Although the results aren't in yet, I'm happy to see that the faculty have come up with something that makes sense, that they accept as their own, and that can easily be tweaked if needed.

Success for the new sequences will be defined by how well students do in the subsequent courses and by how many students graduate. If we can shorten the time to completion and actually improve success rates, everybody wins.

New administrators on the scene will have to walk a fine line: they need to call attention to the problem and provide the background conditions in which other people can solve the problem, without directly solving the problem themselves. This takes patience, self-awareness, and self-control, but it's the best route to sustainable success. If the initiative is dictated from above, faculty will drag their feet, and the project will last only as long as the administrator is there and attentive. For the faculty to own it, they have to own it.

Over the long term, of course, it would be lovely if the K–12 system did such a good job that developmental education became entirely unnecessary. But we're not there, and I don't expect us to be there anytime soon.

Intriguingly, in my time at FPU, developmental coursework was nearly nonexistent. All but the very least capable students were placed directly into college-level English, and even developmental math was relatively lightly used. And that wasn't because the students came in particularly strong. It was a policy decision, based on the observation that students don't like to pay for courses that don't count.

Although that made teaching the 100-level courses incredibly frustrating, it did lead to a much higher graduation rate than that of any of the local community colleges. That's consistent with research by Nikki Edgecombe (2011) of the Community College Research Center, who studied the Virginia community college system and its experience with "noncompliers." Virginia's system gives students placement tests upon arrival, but apparently many students simply ignored the results and signed themselves up for 100-level courses after they were advised to take developmental courses. Edgecombe's findings show that the noncompliers did just as well in the 100-level courses as did those who placed directly into the 100 level. And they saved themselves significant time and money in the process.

The results aren't necessarily conclusive, of course. One could argue that the noncompliers were not a random sample of developmental students. Perhaps they knew that the test was invalid in their case—maybe they were hung over when they took it—so they decided not to give the results undue credence. Or maybe they were just unusually confident. In any event, the sheer number of them—a quarter million over a decade—suggests that the results are more than a fluke.

Whatever the flavor of innovation a given college (or state) chooses, though, this is the rare case in which the work that needs to be done is widely acknowledged and politically popular. The wise young administrator will move the topic of developmental education to the top of the to-do list.

Reaching out to Men

For reasons at which I can only guess, female students are far likelier to complete degrees than are male students. That's true across racial and income categories. (In fact, at my college, Latina women have started outperforming white men in developmental math classes.) Absolute numbers also favor women, although that's largely a matter of age. Among students under age twenty, the gender ratio is close to even. The older the age group, the more female it gets. Men over twenty-five are few and far between in class.

If the popular stereotype of displaced workers seeking retraining were true, we'd expect to see the exact opposite. But for whatever reason—which would take another book to explore—adult men simply don't show up at community college in large numbers. And when they do, they seldom complete their courses of study.

I didn't expect that to be true when I started my career. Coming up through the 1980s and 1990s, I heard about the various ways that women's paths were blocked. (Through my mom's anecdotes, I even got some first-person exposure.) When I was at FPU, the student body was majority male. But in the community college world, men are scarce, and successful men of color even more so.

A leader who develops a way to reach out, successfully, to men of color and men over age twenty-five will be hailed, rightly, as a national hero.

Charging Differential Fees

Pricing is another area that will require serious innovation. This may involve some difficult discussions.

Certain programs and majors cross-subsidize others. Running certain programs on the cheap enables colleges to take much greater losses in others than they could otherwise tolerate. This is especially true in colleges that don't use differential tuition. When the per-credit rate is the same whether applied to a chalk-and-talk lecture section or a small specialized lab class, the only way to sustain the small lab is to run the lecture as a cash cow. With state appropriations declining as percentages of institutional budgets, the need for cross-subsidization only increases.

If a system or college is unwilling to bite the bullet and specialize, a useful intermediate step could be to charge differential fees (or tuition) by program. Let the students in the higher-cost programs pay a slightly higher price for the privilege. It's taking the lab-fees model to another level.

The advantage of this system is that it makes the higher-cost programs more economically sustainable, and it does so without continuing to bleed the liberal arts core. The disadvantages are that the college would still lose money, and higher cost could compromise access. Ultimately, I consider this a weaker alternative to real specialization, but as a political fallback position, it could buy some time.

Colleges have to choose carefully where to lose money. Programs like nursing, engineering, and dental hygiene are usually money pits; the college compensates for that with classes like Intro to Psychology, which can be taught as lectures by adjuncts without much expensive or specialized equipment. There's a compelling argument to be made that the survival of the lecture class, in the face of decades' worth of research showing that it's a poor learning environment, is largely a function of finances. It may not work terribly well as a learning environment, but one adjunct lecturing fifty students without any special equipment is remarkably profitable. In a public college, that profit goes to offset the losses of other, more expensive programs.

Community colleges run those expensive programs for several reasons. They're often very popular with the public or with local politicians. Students often get jobs. Student demand is strong. Public expectations include certain programs with clear, short-term job market payoff. When employer demand is strong enough, as in certain health care and technology programs at certain times, it's possible to get subventions from employers to help offset the costs. And at a really basic level, the communities that community colleges are supposed to serve often need those programs. If you shut down every community college nursing program that loses money, you will have a vicious shortage of nurses in short order.

Whatever specialization a college chooses, it needs to be sustainable. With states increasingly shirking their role as partners, and with students already struggling to make student loan payments, the wise administrator will seek other partners to help offset burdens and make the college effective.

Leveraging and Expanding Partnerships

At the community college level, several kinds of partnerships are already common. A more robust series of interinstitutional partnerships would help ensure the survival of broadly available higher education.

HIGH SCHOOL PARTNERSHIPS

These are usually called "dual-enrollment" programs. In dual-enrollment programs, high school–age students take a mix of courses and get both high school and college credit simultaneously. These programs come in several varieties.

The classic version of dual enrollment involves the high school student who happens to be a math prodigy and has hit the curricular ceiling in math at the public school long before graduation. That student might stay in high school for other subjects, but attend the local community college for, say, differential equations. But over the last decade, several other varieties of dual enrollment have become common.

In states with large homeschool communities, it's becoming common for groups of parents to contract with a local community college to give their children access to classes they couldn't teach well themselves, such as foreign languages or lab sciences.

But the biggest shift over the last decade has been the transformation of dual enrollment from a safety valve for high achievers to a method of dropout prevention for marginal students. For example, as mentioned in an earlier chapter, in the Gateway to College program, sponsored by the Bill and Melinda Gates Foundation, at-risk high school students take college-level English classes on a college campus and get concurrent high school credit for it. The idea is to give at-risk students a taste of the college experience and to show them by direct experience that they can handle it. It's designed to give them both a goal—a college degree—and a head start on achieving that goal.

In my observation, programs that follow the Gateway model both solve and create issues.

Depending on how the participating students are selected and mentored, programs like these can make positive differences for the students involved. On my own campus, I had a discussion with a Gateway student who confided that high school was hell for him and that escaping that environment—and replacing it with the community college—saved his life. He identified as gay, and presented himself in a way that was consistent with some popular stereotypes; as a result, he said, he was constantly taunted, beaten up, and generally made to live in fear in high school. When he got to the college campus, there was none of that, and he was finally able to let his guard down and just be a student. For students like him, the issue in high school wasn't academic ability, even though his high school grades were low; it was the culture of the school. Escaping that culture made a palpable difference in the quality of both his life and his work.

That said, though, programs like these on college campuses don't always sit well with the faculty, who see them as eroding the identity of the institution. From that perspective, there's nothing wrong with taking in the occasional high achiever, as that's premised on recognizing that college is qualitatively different—academically harder—than high school. But bringing in students who were barely cutting it in high school seems to play into the stereotype of community college as thirteenth grade.

What's difficult about this objection is that it doesn't readily admit to arguments based on evidence. When the local dual-enrollment program posted astonishingly good pass rates in college classes for its students—better than the overall college population, in fact—many faculty were unimpressed. Their objection wasn't that it couldn't be done; it was that it shouldn't be done. It violated their sense of who they were as college faculty. Arguments from identity require an entirely different kind of response.

Finally, in many states, the path of dual enrollment leads right back into the high school itself. There, the local community college shares curriculum with the local high schools, who task their own teachers to teach the college curriculum during the regular school day, offering dual credit. (This arrangement is usually called concurrent enrollment, as opposed to dual enrollment.) In a sense, this is a variation on the traditional Advanced Placement class. The chief advantage to the student is that transcripted credits often carry more weight in transfer than do AP or IB (International Baccalaureate) credits.

As problematic as Gateway-style programs can be, though, concurrent-enrollment programs strike me as far worse. In Gateway-style programs, the students are taking classes with college faculty (and usually with traditional college students) on campus. In concurrent-enrollment programs, by contrast, the students go from third-period French to fourth-period college to fifth-period social studies. The interaction in class is no different than in a high school class, and the teachers are high school teachers. And unlike an AP class, there's no nationally normed test at the end to keep everyone honest. Although it's probably possible to run large-scale programs like this and do it well, the gravitational pull to water down the academic standards would be constant.

INDUSTRY PARTNERSHIPS Many community colleges form programs (either credit or noncredit) in conjunction with local employers, either to prepare students to become employees or to help incumbent employees maintain or improve their skill levels. Although some of these partnerships emerge locally and organically, they're increasingly organized under the aegis of a federal workforce development grant. Such "public-private partnerships" are intended to create mutually beneficial outcomes, and sometimes they do, although the administrative cost of these programs tends to be remarkably high when compared to traditional academic offerings. (That's because every grant has to have its own project director.) Courses taught under this umbrella can range from specific technical applications to English as a Second Language.

SOCIAL SERVICE AGENCY PARTNERSHIPS The concept is similar to industry partnerships. For example, many community colleges have contracts with area Head Start programs to help train their teachers. In practice, many workforce programs are actually tripartite agreements among social service agencies, local employers, and community colleges.

ARTICULATION AGREEMENTS These are formal agreements between individual colleges, or sometimes groups of colleges, to accept each other's credits. The classic example is an agreement between a community college and a four-year college to allow students who graduate the community college with an associate's degree to start at the four-year college with full junior standing. The benefit to the student is a four-year degree with two years paid at the community college tuition rate, which typically results in much lower student debt.

In practice, articulation agreements are more complex than that. They have to address individual majors, quirky local requirements, reverse transfers, minimum grade levels, general education requirements, and more.

These agreements are all helpful, as far as they go, and I expect to see more of them. But some other models are also starting to emerge, and this is where I expect to see the most significant changes.

On-Site Articulations I haven't seen a formal term for these, but they are arrangements in which a four-year college contracts with a community college to offer a bachelor's degree completion program on the community college's campus. The appeal to students is that they know the campus, they're already comfortable with the environment, and they often receive additional transfer credits beyond the traditional two years, which reduces their overall expenses.

In some ways, these are traditional "dual-admission" programs, taken to the next level. Under a dual-admission program, a student enrolls at Smith Community College and declares upon enrollment that she intends to transfer eventually to Jones State University. Jones State guarantees her eventual admission, as long as the student completes a given course of study with a specified minimum GPA.

In the on-site articulations, as I'm calling them, the transfer to Jones State still happens, but Jones State actually teaches the classes on the Smith Community College campus. The idea is to facilitate a seamless transition for students by allowing them to continue to go to a place where they're already comfortable.

These courses are usually offered during evenings or weekends, to cater to working adults. The target population is usually working adults who have two-year degrees but who need more to move up at work. These programs appeal to community colleges in several ways: they offer revenue from additional transfer courses, revenue from room rental, the marketing appeal of being able to complete a degree there, and the legibility to students of a path beyond the associate's. The programs appeal to four-year colleges by providing access to additional students they otherwise would not have reached, as well as considerable savings on infrastructure, as they don't have to build anything to increase capacity.

Community College Bachelor's Degrees Several states allow these now, at least in selected fields. It's a variation on the on-site articulation, except without the second college. In Florida, for example, community colleges are allowed to grant bachelor's degrees in several fields that the state legislature has decided need extra staffing help, such as teacher education.

I'll admit some wariness here. Part of what makes community colleges unique is their specificity of mission: they stop after the sophomore year. Colleges wanting to be universities, and comprehensive universities that strive for elite status—this is the "vertical mission creep" I mentioned earlier. When a college that's already pursuing one mission decides to add another, there's a real danger of loss of focus, and of spreading resources too thin. My preference is to do one mission well rather than two missions poorly.

Still, the momentum on the ground is substantial, and I have to concede that this approach certainly offers both convenience and legibility for students.

ALTERNATE CERTIFICATIONS Until now, most of the dialogue about improving student outcomes in college have assumed that there are many paths but only one destination: a traditional degree. It may be time to explore other destinations.

Occupational certificates have a long history in community colleges, but they've usually been treated as afterthoughts or sidelines. A rigid internal distinction between "credit-bearing" and "noncredit" programs— which has consequences for financial aid eligibility, graduation rates, and accreditation—keeps the two areas from speaking to each other.

But the argument for keeping the two separate is becoming harder to sustain. Some of the most exciting innovations now involve "scaffolding" noncredit programs so that they carry some weight toward degrees. The idea is to recognize the value of what was learned on the noncredit side. For example, at my college, students in the Allied Health track receive three credits if they come in with a CNA certification.

"Credit for prior learning," such as CAEL provides, can also offer adults with skills they've picked up along the way—usually at work—some recognition of what they've done, the better to encourage them to continue toward a degree.

Certificates can be way stations toward a degree, or supplements to a degree, or just freestanding. They probably won't mean much at the high end of the scale, but at the low end, they offer someone with limited time a more positive alternative to just dropping out.

At this point, alternatives to the degree face some serious obstacles. Credit for prior learning, for example, still carries a whiff of "life experience credit," the classic expedient of the diploma mill. (CAEL's model, which relies on documented competencies, is much more than just "life experience," but the reputation remains.) The financial aid system is still built for degrees and has trouble handling certificates. I saw this myself when the first round of "Gainful Employment" regulations came out, and colleges had to compile and publish statistics on degree or certificate completion and starting salaries. We had a number of certificates that students picked up on the way to degrees, sometimes intentionally, sometimes not. When a student picked up a certificate on the side, as an afterthought, sometimes the "time to completion" seemed out of proportion to the number of credits. That's what happens with afterthoughts.

Finally, of course, employers and the outside world often don't know how to weigh certificates. HR departments will frequently use a degree as an initial screen on job postings to winnow down candidate pools. It's a blunt instrument, but as long as everyone (mostly) agrees on what a degree is, the requirement offers a first-level approximation of the skill level involved in the position. If significant numbers of people start showing up with various certificates instead, HR departments will have to become more discerning in how to calibrate the value of certificates. I'd guess that in the early going, some quality people would get screened out for lacking a "degree," which could lead to delayed acceptance of certificates by students. But over the long term, the appeal of a more customized bundle of postsecondary courses strikes me as too powerful to ignore.

PARTNERSHIPS WITH DOCTORAL UNIVERSITIES These have been slow to launch, though the argument for them strikes me as obvious. Doctorate-granting universities have, as part of their mission, an obligation to train graduate students for academic careers. Given that more institutions are teaching oriented than research oriented, teaching experience in a community college or similar institution can give an applicant an advantage.

Still, in most cases, graduate students who teach at community colleges do so on their own initiative, with no support from their home institution.

Where geography permits, I can see an argument for a visiting teaching fellowship arrangement between a research university and a nearby community college. For the cost of some limited mentoring, the two institutions could essentially build community college teaching into the TA experience of graduate students. This arrangement would help the finances of the doctoral universities, which often can't afford to fund their graduate students to completion (with predictable consequences for completion rates). It would also help community colleges gain access to recently trained, enthusiastic instructors, with less moral ambiguity than attends the adjunct arrangement.

The systemic benefit for higher education as a whole would be a more realistic training regimen for the next generation of college faculty. Instead of the current dysfunctional system, in which people are socialized into the expectations of research universities and then loosed upon teaching colleges, where they experience chronic frustration and disappointment, rising young faculty could learn early on the realities of the institutions at which most of them will eventually work. Some might be turned off by it, but that's not necessarily bad; if they hate to teach, better to find out early. Others might discover that a sector they had previously given little thought actually holds real appeal. That strikes me as a real, and low-cost, gain for education as a whole.

Finding Alternative Funding

The current default funding model for community colleges has operating funds coming from only two (or sometimes three) sources: the state, students, and sometimes the county or service area. That limited set of funding streams is supposed to support the entire range of programs and services at the college. Given that even a medium-size community college will easily have over a hundred degree options, in addition to a full range of student services, the funding inevitably gets spread thin. As I discussed earlier, over time, colleges have to choose between running fewer programs and watering down the programs they have; typically, they choose the latter, going with adjuncts to save money.

The more successful universities, though, don't follow this model. Instead, they've diversified their funding streams in order to reduce their dependence on any single one. Given the continued struggles for state funding, and the reality of student loan burdens, this strategy strikes me as wise, and worth emulating.

Many public universities draw funding from sources ranging from facility use fees to technology transfer to logo licensing. Although each source has its own strings attached, the diversity of sources (and therefore of strings) means that if any one source sours, it will have only a limited impact.

Revisiting Philanthropy

Some older colleges and the more prestigious universities have long relied heavily on philanthropic giving as a revenue source. (This is one area in which for-profits simply cannot compete.) But many community colleges are now becoming more serious about courting philanthropy. This development was born of necessity, but it's a positive one anyway; a more diversified funding stream allows for greater operational autonomy.

Philanthropy has benefits that go beyond immediate dollar signs. It also builds relationships with the kinds of people who have considerable sway with state legislatures. When some wealthy and powerful pillars of the community feel a direct affinity with the local community college, that college gains allies it can call on in difficult times. This is not to be discounted.

I expect to see community colleges taking a more thoughtful approach to philanthropy in the next decade. With state appropriations likely to lag for some time, and with large-scale tuition increases politically difficult, it would be irresponsible not to.

The folks who do fundraising for nonprofits—the "development" community—are already starting to take more notice of community colleges. The Council for Advancement and Support of Education (CASE), for example, held its first national conference on community college fundraising in 2012. This is good news for community colleges, though the learning curve will be steep.

The people who do fundraising for a living like to say that "fundraising is friendraising." Leaving aside the crime against the English language, it's certainly true that it would be a mistake to reduce fundraising to getting the largest checks possible. For a college that intends to stick around a while, the goal should be to play the long game, which means building relationships over time.

Those relationships can take a number of positive forms. For example, many highly successful people, once they reach a certain stage in life, like to mentor younger people. A college is a natural setting for that to happen; it's full of younger people looking for guidance, and mentoring is a form of education in itself. Connecting successful people who like to share their insights with younger people who are just starting out and looking for guidance is a win for everybody. That's especially true for students who come from backgrounds in which successful role models were relatively scarce. Mentors can help students learn some of the unwritten rules of success in ways that traditional classes sometimes can't, particularly in areas like entrepreneurship.

Long-term connections with successful people can help a college politically as well. In navigating the thickets of local politics in which everybody knows everybody, having some prominent local figures on your side can make the difference between success and failure.

Local boards of trustees present excellent recruitment opportunities for prominent local figures, and they can cement the kind of long-term relationships that results in both direct philanthropy and other, less obvious forms of help. When important local people feel a direct stake in the success of the community college, they tend to offer their help when they can. They also often ensure that their own organizations are receptive to local graduates, which makes far more of a difference at the community college level than at most four-year schools. (Community college students who don't transfer upon graduation tend to stay local.)

Thinking in terms of friendraising has been optional for the founding generation of community college leaders, but it will be mandatory for the next cohort. With states continuing to pull back from their historic roles, the skills and inclinations to recruit and maintain allies will become all the more important. This is one area in which community colleges have a competitive advantage over for-profits, if they're willing to step up.

Friendraising often works indirectly. Personal enrichment classes that don't necessarily turn a profit can be long-term investments in the college, if they attract the right clientele. One college at which I worked had Senior Day every spring, for which it would recruit busloads of senior citizens from local seniors' centers and put on a day of programming on topics of interest to them. (The big draws were typically gardening, musical theater, and politics.) Senior Day was a lot of fun in its own right, but part of its purpose was to give a powerful local voting bloc a sense that the college had something to offer them. Simply getting different groups of people physically on campus for different events was a way of starting to build relationships.

Of course, as mentioned in Chapter Two, direct giving usually doesn't have a direct impact on the operating budget, as community colleges typically aren't able to devote donations to operations. Because they don't have endowments that generate investment income for operations, there isn't even the indirect effect that many four-year colleges and universities are able to enjoy.

Conceptually, at least, this doesn't have to be true. If community colleges were allowed to establish endowments, it's at least possible that at some point—after hitting a critical mass of giving—some investment income could make its way into the operating budget. But even without that, which is very much a long-term strategy, it may be possible to offset certain kinds of operating costs with philanthropy. If donations can be used to support lab equipment, for example, then the operating money that would have gone for lab equipment is available for other things. Some colleges have a Center for Teaching Excellence, funded by donors, that offers mini-grants for faculty and staff professional development; to the extent that mini-grants can offset travel funds, all the better.

Foundations and philanthropic giving are still badly underdeveloped at the community college level, relative to private four-year colleges and universities. The next generation of leaders simply will not have the option of continuing to ignore or soft-pedal the importance of recruiting allies and donors.

The Choice: Evolve or Decline

The world is changing, and the demands on community colleges are changing right along with it. I advise administrators who are looking to their short-term career goals to pick their battles carefully, as many of the changes I suggest here will provoke tremendous political opposition on campus if raised there. Stationary inertia is powerful within any public institution, and community colleges certainly have their share. Over time, though, failing to raise the issues is a choice in itself. If we fail to confront those changes and help the institution evolve, at best we might hang on, doing everything just a little bit worse every year.

For community college administrators, the goal is to embrace the best elements of change without losing sight of the mission. That means, among other things, embracing the enhanced transparency offered by electronic communication, and turning it into a tool for crowdsourcing ideas. It means letting go of the old comprehensive model founded on geographical scarcity, and embracing the efficiencies offered by the Internet and regional models. It means finally jettisoning the premodern notion of the faculty role and replacing it with a conception of faculty as creative professionals whose job it is to help students learn. It means doubling down on what community colleges do best: providing students with an academic support structure, teaching the evergreen disciplines, and keeping a laserlike focus on the first two years. It means moving past the credit hour and the traditional calendar. And perhaps most important, it involves creating campus climates in which constructive experimentation is rewarded and internal politicking is not.

The model I propose is not a for-profit business, nor a return to a Golden Age, nor the present but with more money. It's an attempt to remake community colleges in rational and fair ways that will allow them to continue to fulfill their mission as the world continues to change. The mission is too important to let slip behind unconscious habit or short-term convenience.

CONCLUSION

THE NEXT COHORT OF COMMUNITY COLLEGE LEADERS will have a full plate.

First, it's not obvious where these leaders will come from. When colleges essentially skipped a generation of full-time faculty hires in favor of adjuncts, they did so on the basis of a short-term calculation of cost. But that ignored succession planning. When you skip a generation and the time comes for that generation to step up, you have a problem.

Some colleges and professional groups are belatedly starting leadership development programs, hoping to make the most of the relatively few people they actually hired. That's helpful as far as it goes, but it's unlikely to fill the whole gap.

Assuming that good people are found, though, the tasks have changed.

Public demands on community colleges are higher than they have ever been, both in terms of enrollments and in terms of political expectations. But public funding is lower, and the funding that does exist is channeled directly through students. The gravitational pull of higher tuition is becoming progressively stronger. Ironically enough, some of that pull comes from scholarships and financial aid. To the extent that money is funneled through students, the only way for colleges to get that money is to charge students as much as possible.

Community colleges are facing financial challenges much more severe than they have in the past, and that's saying something. On the revenue side, public funding is under sustained assault, and students can't keep paying higher tuition when the real income of the young is actually falling. On the cost side, Baumol's cost disease (see note 1 for Chapter Two) is insidious, and the combination of life tenure, no mandatory retirement, and seniority-driven raises pushes inexorably in one direction. Colleges will have to keep up with the technology used in the occupations for which students are trained, which means they'll have to continue to invest in technology even when it doesn't save money. As labor-intensive institutions, colleges will experience increasing pressure from the continuing spiral of health insurance costs. Online education will continue to wreak havoc with the concept of the geographically defined service area, with likely implications for local political support.

Internally, constituencies who feel threatened are likelier to circle the wagons than to engage in forward-looking discussions of adaptation and alternatives. Some will take a shoot-the-messenger approach to any new leader who dares to speak the truth. Others will simply drag their feet, hoping to ride out the clock before the whole thing collapses.

It won't be easy.

But leaders who are willing to come to grips with the reality of the situation have never been more necessary. If the next generation fails to step up, community colleges will continue along their default path. As I see it, that doesn't lead anywhere good.

The Default Paths

If nothing is done, community colleges across the nation will go one of two routes. Either they'll raise prices enough to cover costs and basically become private, or they'll decline in size and relevance to become once again the afterthoughts of higher education.

The first path, raising prices, at least allows for the maintenance of quality. But it defeats the purpose of having public institutions in the first place, which is to offer accessibility for people who can't afford private alternatives. The second path would sacrifice quality in the name of cost control. That path also gradually removes the institution's reason to exist, and it also carries the real political risk of increasing the identification of community colleges with the least powerful people in society. In the United States, for reasons many and shameful, institutions or programs dedicated to the poor are made poor themselves. This is not a politically sustainable path.

California has taken a different approach. There, community colleges have maintained quality and low cost by stubbornly staying as small as their appropriations. The larger districts have waiting lists in the tens of thousands in any given year, and it's a crapshoot for each student as to whether she'll be able to get the classes needed for graduation. The choice there has been to sacrifice accessibility, thereby creating a huge and growing opening for for-profits to redefine the entire market. Students who are shut out, whether in whole or in part, will find other ways, and they'll pay for the privilege. Or they won't, and the overall education level of the population will decline. Or, in the likeliest of all worlds, both outcomes will occur to some extent, and the state will have a lower educational level without any actual savings.

Conscious Choice

I'd much rather see the next generation change the terms of the discussion. If these leaders make a conscious choice to sacrifice many of the current institutional rigidities, they may be able to maintain and even improve the fulfillment of the mission.

Must we remain wedded to the credit hour? Does tenure still make sense, assuming it once did? Must every campus offer every program? How can technology actually help with costs, rather than just growing as a line item year after year? What are the unique contributions community colleges are best situated to make? What can or should be left to the for-profits, now that they're too big to ignore? Are there ways to address insufficient academic preparation without the multisemester death march that characterizes most developmental education? And how can we tap into the creativity of the faculty, rather than just treating them as cost items or inputs?

More basically, if community colleges are going to adapt to the new realities, they'll have to move to adaptation as a conscious choice. This will take audacious leadership.

In a fear-based culture, it's easy to read failure as confirmation of fatalism. The "I told you so" chorus is quick to jump on any sign that a particular program or policy didn't work. And in a fear-based setting rich with legalisms and long-embittered but immovable people, getting past that attitude is a tall order.

But the alternative to experimentation is atrophy and decay. The last few decades have demonstrated that amply. The alternative to risk-taking is not safety; it's decline.

At the outset, I defined the job of administration as setting the background conditions in which faculty and staff could do their best work. Whereas many of those conditions are relatively concrete—facilities, funding, policies that don't crash into each other or create perverse incentives—some of them are softer. They're about climate.

Climate Change

The best chance for positive change, I suspect, lies in drawing on the collective intelligence of everyone involved in higher education. Locally, that absolutely includes the faculty—both part-time and full-time—as well as staff and administration. Getting that positive change to work without falling into the old habits of credential worship or conflict avoidance will take real skill.

Doing that will involve tremendous self-restraint, paradoxically enough. A mercurial leader, or one who simply accepts whatever the national flavor of the month happens to be, does not inspire trust. Nor does one who solicits input, disregards it, and then moves forward with what he obviously wanted in the first place.

Ego is the enemy. If a leader is willing to defer to a better idea or to facts that suggest that her idea is misplaced, then she creates a climate in which truth trumps rank. She adopts the position of the scientist, deferring to the results of experiments as they happen.

The key difference is that she isn't always—or even usually—the one actually running the experiments. She establishes the background conditions that make productive experiments possible, and honors the results when the faculty and staff design and run those experiments. She might ask the questions—which takes no small amount of courage in itself—but then lets the results speak. And if that means admitting when she got something wrong, then that's what it means.

It's much easier to trust someone who is capable of admitting a mistake. Making it possible to do that without committing career suicide involves setting a climate in which the "I told you so" chorus isn't too powerful and in which not trying is considered worse than failing.

I've had some luck with using both synchronous (meetings) and asynchronous (blogs) formats for on-campus formative discussions of new proposals. The word "formative" is key. If the proposal is presented as a fait accompli and the announcements are merely sales jobs, the usual cynicism will result. But if people have a chance to weigh in at a stage when their input actually matters—and, better, if they can see the proposal shift as a direct result of their input—you're likelier to get better proposals and more support at the same time.

The trick will be in conveying a sense of urgency about the big picture, while resisting the temptation to be too controlling about the results. Because the big picture is urgent and getting more so.

At a really basic level, community colleges are public institutions. They draw on the public purse to serve a public purpose. That language is getting lost in our politics; we've gone so far down the road of user fees and DIY that we've nearly forgotten the point of public institutions. They exist to serve the weak and to protect the weak against the predations of the strong.

That kind of protection is the point. When the institutional form of that protection has become dysfunctional or unsustainable, defending it doesn't help. We need to be willing to experiment with different forms. I look forward to trying.

NOTES

CHAPTER 2

1. Economists call this Baumol's disease, after William Baumol, who wrote about it in the 1960s. He noted that it takes just as many musicians, and just as long, to play a Beethoven string quartet now as it did a hundred years ago; the net productivity increase is zero. But we don't pay musicians what we paid them a hundred years ago. They're paid more than that, or there would be no working musicians. Put differently, their pay increases have outstripped their productivity increases for a very long time, and there's no end in sight.

2. Perversely, successful medical outcomes can actually drive up costs over time, as people who once would have died of heart attacks in their fifties now live long enough to die possibly more expensively of cancer in their seventies.

3. I'll add a recommendation, one based on direct observation: never say yes to "temporary" trailers. Once they're there, they'll never go away. The temptation of "just one more year" will go on until they fall apart.

4. Perkins is a federal grant geared toward employment-focused programs: vocational or technical education.

5. Of course, pricing in higher ed works in funny ways anyway. Education can be seen as a prestige good with ambiguous measures of quality, but people outside the club often take price as a rough indicator of quality. If you get what you pay for, and you don't have to pay very much, what are you getting? Community colleges are painfully aware of this, because as the low-cost providers, we get stigmatized. In a market in which the "Chivas Regal effect" is paramount, pricing discipline can actually backfire.

6. Gifts can sometimes generate new costs of their own, as in the case of "challenge" or "matching" gifts, in which a donor offers to pay some set portion of a given cost on the condition that others (whether other donors or the college budget) pay the rest. I've actually seen colleges turn down gifts because the matching requirements were too heavy.

CHAPTER 3

1.   There are exceptions to that. Conceivably, if the released time were substantial and permanent, you'd have to hire someone full-time. And in some states, like Massachusetts, tuition for courses taught by full-timers is accounted differently than tuition for courses taught by adjuncts. But the basic point still stands.

2.   The American Association of University Professors (AAUP) quixotically claims that colleges can't lay off tenured faculty just because the programs in which they teach no longer exist. The AAUP is alone in this and, in my estimation, fundamentally wrong. Salaries are in exchange for services performed. If the services are no longer performable, there's no longer an argument for the salaries.

CHAPTER 4

1.   For a nice history of the emergence of the independent contractor ideal, see Riesman and Jencks, *The Academic Revolution* (New Brunswick, NJ: Transaction Press, 2001; originally published 1968).

2.   I always smile ruefully whenever I read a management book that talks about weeding out the problem employees. In tenured and unionized academia, problem employees typically outlast their managers. It's not at all unusual for tenured faculty to last four decades or more. In my first deanship, I attended several retirement functions for faculty who had started working there before I was born.

3.   To make it more concrete: when I arrived in 2003, the "kid" in the Sociology Department had been hired in 1975. The college hadn't hired a political scientist since 1970. The second-youngest member of the English Department, which had twenty-something full-timers in it, was in her late forties.

CHAPTER 5

1.   Some larger colleges employ a provost model. The provost is largely the COO to the president's CEO. The provost is basically second in command, and chief of all things internal. In my observation, most single-campus community colleges don't use the provost model.

2.   This becomes painfully clear in colleges with "diversity requirements" in certain curricula. Where there's a requirement that a student take at least x number of credits from a list of courses that have been "diversity certified," you can bet that departments will do whatever they can to make sure that their own courses are on that list. In the absence of some really specific criteria, I'd expect to see that list expand quickly and in some pretty counterintuitive ways.

3. In my time on faculty at FPU, we were frequently told that the college didn't recoup its recruiting costs until the student paid for a second trimester. Whether that was true, I don't know, but it circulated widely. I never really understood what I, as an instructor, was supposed to do with that information, and I was lucky that my dean never pressed the point. I've never heard anything like that on the community college side.

4. Although women have actually become a majority of the administrators in community colleges across the United States, mothers of school-age (or younger) children are still relatively rare among their ranks. And men whose expectations of parenting were formed by their own working moms—and whose relationships are founded, in part, on those expectations—aren't going to be as quick to devote every waking hour to being out of the house.

CHAPTER 6

1. Oddly, traditional higher ed has been much more circumspect about the real scandal, which is accreditation buying. For reasons that passeth understanding, the various regional accreditors have allowed nonprofit colleges to simply transfer their accreditations to for-profit buyers, even when the mission changes fundamentally. This apparent confusion of accreditation with taxi licenses is inexcusable on any rational grounds, though it attracts much less criticism than other, more defensible habits of the industry. I suspect that that's because the alternative—outright closures of colleges—strikes a little close to home.

2. Some for-profits are actually leaders in outcomes assessment. Because they live and die by employability, they need to ensure that their graduates are actually capable of doing what the institution says they're capable of doing. They offer few programs per campus, so it's relatively easy to get good sample sizes, and with multiple campuses over multiple states, it's relatively easy to filter out local quirks. Done badly, of course, outcomes assessment can lead to idiotic standardization, but done well, there's real value in it.

REFERENCES

Angus, Jeff. *Management by Baseball*. New York: Harper Business, 2006.

Barber, Benjamin. *An Aristocracy of Everyone*. New York: Oxford University Press, 1992.

Bowen, William, and Julie Sosa. *Prospects for Faculty in the Arts and Sciences*. New York: Princeton University Press, 1989.

Burns, Ken (Creator). *Baseball*. Washington, D.C.: Public Broadcasting System, 1994. Film.

Cauchon, Dennis. "Student Loans Outstanding Will Exceed $1 Trillion This Year." *USA Today*, October 25, 2011. http://www.usatoday.com/money/perfi/college/story/2011-10-19/student-loan-debt/50818676/1.

Cohen, Arthur, and Florence Brawer. *The American Community College*. (5th ed.) San Francisco: Jossey-Bass, 2008.

Collins, Jim. *Good to Great*. New York: HarperBusiness, 2001.

Complete College America. *Time Is the Enemy*. Washington, DC: Complete College America, 2011.

Cook, Bryan, and Young Kim. *The American College President 2012*. Washington, DC: ACE Center for Policy Analysis, 2012.

Edgecombe, Nikki. "Accelerating the Academic Achievement of Students Referred to Developmental Education." New York: Community College Research Center, 2011.

Gordon, Robert. "Revisiting U.S. Productivity Growth over the Past Century with a View of the Future." NBER Working Paper 15834. Cambridge, MA: National Bureau of Economic Research, March 2010.

Gunsalus, C. K. *The College Administrator's Survival Guide*. New York: Harvard University Press, 2006.

Jacobs, Joanne. "Some Teens Start College Work Early via Dual Enrollment." *U.S. News and World Report*, March 9, 2012. http://www.usnews.com/education/best-colleges/articles/2012/03/09/some-teens-start-college-work-early-via-dual-enrollment.

Jaschik, Scott. "Administrators' Salaries Up 4%." *Insidehighered.com*. February 26, 2007. http://www.insidehighered.com/news/2007/02/26/salaries.

Jones, Del. "Let people know where they stand, Welch says." *USA Today*, April 18, 2005. http://usatoday30.usatoday.com/educate/college/careers/Advice /advice4-18-05.htm.

Kiley, Kevin. "The Other Debt Crisis." *Insidehighered.com*. April 10, 2012. http://www.insidehighered.com/news/2012/04/10/public-universities-will -take-more-debt-states-decrease-spending-capital-projects.

Kübler-Ross, Elisabeth. *On Death and Dying*. New York: Scribner, 1997. (Originally published 1969)

Murray, Alan. "Should I Rank My Employees?" *The Wall Street Journal*, retrieved November 9, 2012. http://guides.wsj.com/management /recruiting-hiring-and-firing/should-i-rank-my-employees/.

Nocera, Joe. "Why We Need For-Profit Colleges." *New York Times*, September 16, 2011. http://www.nytimes.com/2011/09/18/magazine/ why-we-need-for-profit-colleges.html.

Riesman, David, and Christopher Jencks. *The Academic Revolution*. New Brunswick, NJ: Transaction Press, 2001. (Originally published 1968)

Roksa, Josipa, Davis Jenkins, Shanna Smith Jaggars, Matthew Zeidenberg, and Sung-Woo Cho. "Strategies for Promoting Gatekeeper Course Success Among Students Needing Remediation: Research Report for the Virginia Community College System." New York: Community College Research Center, 2009.

Sutton, Robert. *The No Asshole Rule*. New York: Business Plus, 2007.

Vaughan, George B. *The Community College Story*. Washington, DC: American Association of Community Colleges, 2006.

Warner, Gregory. "Putting a Price on Your Pet's Health." *Marketplace Money* podcast, February 17, 2012. http://www.marketplace.org/topics/ your-money/putting-price-your-pets-health.

INDEX